# TREASURY OF
# QUILTING PATTERNS

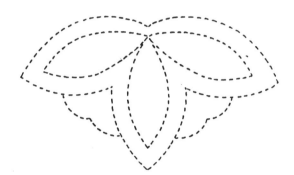

## Cheryl Fall

**STERLING PUBLISHING CO., INC.**
NEW YORK

**Library of Congress Cataloging-in-Publication Data**

Fall, Cheryl.
    Treasury of quilting patterns / by Cheryl Fall.
      p.  cm.
    Includes index.
    ISBN 0-8069-1272-3
    1. Quilting—Patterns.  I. Title.
TT835.F338   1994
746.46'041—dc20            94-30299
                              CIP

10  9  8  7  6  5  4  3  2  1

Published by Sterling Publishing Company, Inc.
387 Park Avenue South, New York, N.Y. 10016
© 1994 by Cheryl Fall
Distributed in Canada by Sterling Publishing
% Canadian Manda Group, One Atlantic Avenue, Suite 105
Toronto, Ontario, Canada M6K 3E7
Distributed in Great Britain and Europe by Cassell PLC
Villiers House, 41/47 Strand, London WC2N 5JE, England
Distributed in Australia by Capricorn Link (Australia) Pty Ltd.
P.O. Box 6651, Baulkham Hills, Business Centre, NSW 2153, Australia
*Manufactured in the United States of America*
*All rights reserved*

Sterling ISBN 0-8069-1272-3

Cover photograph by Nancy Palubniak

# Contents

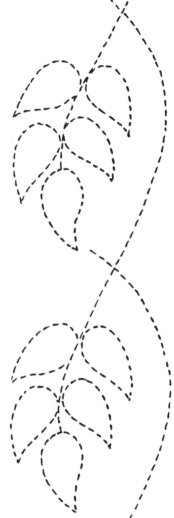

# General Directions

## Marking Tools

Most quilting and fabric stores carry a wide range of marking pens or pencils for quilters. When choosing a marker, bear in mind the color of the fabric you will be marking. However, NEVER, NEVER, NEVER use a #2 graphite pencil!

For dark-colored fabrics, choose a pencil with white, silver, or yellow lead or a washable marker. I prefer to use a silver marking pencil specially designed for marking fabric, which is widely available and is easy to wash out. Also try a white tailor's chalk pencil or a yellow pencil made for marking blueprints, available at art supply stores. If all else fails, try a narrow sliver of mild soap, just like great-grandmother did!

To mark light-colored fabrics, try a silver or white marker, or a blue tailor's chalk pencil. Several marking tools that use powdered chalk also are available. One has a tiny wheel that distributes chalk as it is rolled, which is very handy for marking large areas for "filler" (background) quilting. Other marking devices that use powdered chalk are a bit more difficult to use, but are worth a try.

Some fabric stores also carry felt-tipped pens in either blue or purple ink that is supposed to dissolve in cold water. These pens should not be used as they can start a chemical reaction in the fabric that can cause it to break down at a later date. Also avoid the felt-tipped pens whose ink is supposed to be "air-erasable."

5

After selecting your marking tool, be sure to test it on a swatch of fabric *before* marking your quilt top. Mark a few lines on a scrap of the same fabric as you are using in the quilt, and wash the scrap as you would the finished quilt. Did the markings come out after one washing? I hope so. If not, try a different marking tool instead.

## Using the Patterns in This Book

As you look at the quilting patterns in this book, you will notice that many of them have units that can be put together to make interesting border and block arrangements. I designed them this way because I wanted to give you as many options as possible for your quilts.

For most border designs, you will notice a corner unit. This fits at the end of one of the border units, allowing you to turn the corners of the borders smoothly, without interrupting the flow of the design (Fig. 1). You will also notice that some of the designs have open areas in the center. You can use one of these empty areas for signing and dating your quilt, or for personalizing it with the name of the recipient (Fig. 2).

The designs are given in different sizes. This gives you flexibility as you may have a quilt with plain squares that are 14 inches across, as well as pieced or appliquéd squares with smaller open areas that require some special quilting. Your quilt may have an inner border or block sashing that is 2 or 3 inches wide, and a large outer border that may be up to 12 inches wide. Choose an appropriate-sized design to go in each area of the quilt you want to quilt, depending on the size of each area. The kind of batting you use will also affect how far apart you can put the quilting lines. Check the

*1. A border design with a corner unit.*

*2. A quilting design with an open area.*

manufacturer's suggestions on the batting. In general, polyester batting may be quilted with lines further apart than cotton batting, without lumping. Voila! A matched set of quilting designs! Feel free to rearrange the units as you please. I've tried to show you several different options for one design, but the possibilities are unlimited.

## Marking the Quilt Top

To transfer the designs to your quilt top, I offer the following four methods. Please note that methods 1 through 3 need to be done *before* the layers of the quilt have been basted together. The fourth method should be done *after* the layers are basted.

*Method 1:* If you need to transfer a quilting design onto a light-colored fabric, simply lay the quilt top face up over the pattern (either in the book or a photocopy) and trace the design directly onto the right side of the cloth (Fig. 3). This is perhaps the easiest method.

*3. Tracing a pattern directly from a book.*

**bridge**

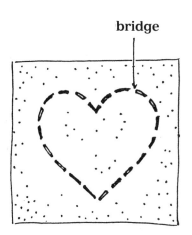

*4. A heart stencil cut in plastic. "Bridges" hold the stencil together.*

*Method 2:* Make a quilting stencil from template-weight plastic or lightweight cardboard. If your plastic is transparent or translucent, trace the quilting design directly onto it with a permanent pen. Cut quilting channels along the marked lines with a sharp knife or an electric stencil cutter. Leave "bridges" (connecting the parts of the stencil) every inch or so to keep the template together (Fig. 4).

*Method 3:* Use a tracing wheel and dressmaker's carbon paper to transfer the designs. First, trace the pattern onto ordinary tracing paper. Align the design on the quilt front where you want it, and place the dressmaker's carbon under the paper, having the colored side against the right side of quilt top. Using the tracing wheel, mark along the lines on the tracing paper to transfer the design (Fig. 5).

*Method 4:* Buy a few yards of a very lightweight stabilizer. Trace the quilting designs onto pieces of the stabilizer and pin or baste these to the already assembled quilt (all the layers are already basted together). Hand- or machine-quilt directly through the stabilizer, and tear it away when you have finished quilting.

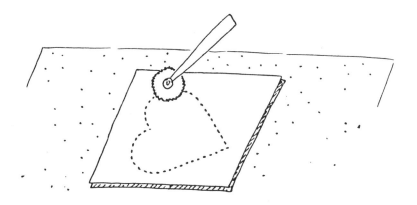

5. *Tracing a pattern with dressmaker's carbon paper.*

When marking your quilt, it's easiest to start with the large areas, such as blocks. When marking the borders, start at the corners and work your way to the center of the border. The reason for this is *balance.* Because every quilt varies, not all of the border patterns given will space themselves perfectly along your borders. If you find that your border patterns do not meet perfectly at the middle, you can stretch or condense the final motif to fit, or use a complementary pattern from the same pattern group, such as a single flower instead of a group of flowers. You may also choose to use this spot for your initials or for personalizing the quilt in some other way.

Always mark your background filler patterns last. The best way to mark these on your quilt top is with a clear plastic ruler. Measure and space your lines of filler pattern evenly.

## Background or Filler Quilting

Filler quilting is an excellent way to fill up large areas of a quilt. It can be very decorative, and also is fun to do.

6. *Echo quilting.*

7. *Stipple quilting.*

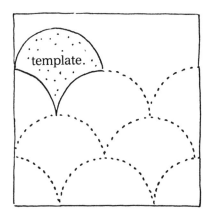

8. *Clamshell fill.*

Echo quilting is one of my favorite methods of filler quilting. This free-motion technique repeats the shape of an appliqué or quilting design in evenly spaced ripples around the shape. These ripples are usually spaced approximately ¼ inch apart and extend all the way to the edges of a quilt block (Fig. 6).

Stippling is another free-motion technique. This technique starts at the edges of a seam or appliqué piece and meanders its way through the area to be quilted. Space the stippling about ⅛ to ¼ inch apart and try not to cross a previous line of quilting; you should not have intersecting lines. The finished results took similar to a jigsaw puzzle (Fig. 7).

Fill designs consist of repeated straight or curved lines. Several patterns for filling are given here: Clamshell (using a saucer or cardboard circle as a template, Fig. 8); cross-hatching (Fig. 9); diamond cross-hatching (Fig. 10); and diagonal lines (Fig. 11). Study your quilt top when choosing the best fill design for your particular project, as it should complement the patchwork pattern, the fabric designs, and the more elaborate quilting motifs that already are used on your quilt.

9. *Cross-hatching.*

10. *Diamond cross-hatching.*

## Basting the Quilt

After deciding on the quilting designs and marking the quilt top, you must assemble the quilt "sandwich" (Fig. 12). If the quilt is very large, you may be able to work on a large table to baste the quilt; if not, you may have to work on the floor. Tape the backing fabric to your work surface with masking tape, with the wrong side of the

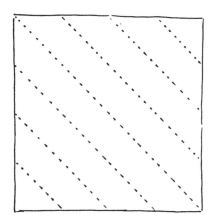

11. *Diagonal lines.*

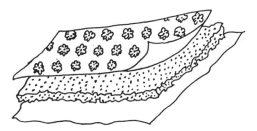

12. *A quilt "sandwich": quilt top, batting, and quilt back.*

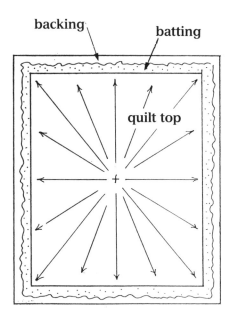

13. *Baste from the center out.*

fabric facing up. Pull slightly at the corners of the backing before taping it, to smooth out any wrinkles in the fabric. Next, center the batting over the backing fabric and trim the batting even with the edges of the backing fabric. Then center the quilt top over the batting. Tape the edges of the quilt top as you did for the backing, smoothing out any wrinkles as you tape.

Hand-baste the layers of the quilt together with thread, or pin baste with small safety pins. Start from the center of your quilt and work outwards towards the edges, smoothing out the wrinkles as you go (Fig. 13). If you are hand-basting, use a basting thread that contrasts in color to your quilt and take very large stitches, which makes it easier to find and remove the basting stitches when you're finished quilting.

If you are pin-basting the layers, try to place the pins in areas that will not be quilted right away, otherwise they will get in your way when you quilt. Never try to sew over pins with your sewing machine—it's dangerous!

After your quilt is basted, secure your quilt in a quilting frame or large hoop if you will be hand quilting. If you use a hoop, start from the center and work outwards. Don't leave the hoop on your work when you are not actually quilting, as it could stretch the fabric. To prepare the quilt for machine quilting, roll the basted quilt in from both sides like the sides of a scroll, leaving a few feet unrolled at the center for you to work on, and secure the rolls with quilt clips. Fold the quilt back and forth on itself like an accordion and place the bulk of it in your lap. Start to machine quilt at the top of the center area, working down towards the part of the quilt nearest you. When you complete the unrolled center area, unroll a bit more to the right, and roll up the excess quilt that you have just quilted on the left roll. Continue in this fashion until you have quilted the entire right roll of the "scroll." Rotate the quilt 180 degrees so that what used to be the left (unquilted) roll is now on the right, and proceed with quilting as before. If you are quilting a diagonal pattern, roll the quilt in from the corners, instead of from end to end, and follow the rest of the above instructions.

## Hand-Quilting Methods

Place your basted quilt "sandwich" of all three layers (backing, batting, and quilt top), with its quilt patterns transferred onto the quilt top, in a large quilter's hoop or quilting frame. Now it's time to start quilting! But before you do, carefully consider what thread you will be using. Hand-quilting thread is a bit heavier than machine sewing thread, and is less likely to tangle. There are several brands of hand-quilting thread on the market, most of which are 100% cotton. If you plan on using just one color of thread for the entire quilt, choose a neutral color that harmonizes well with all the fabrics in the quilt. Or, if you prefer a bolder look, use a contrasting thread. There is no "right" or "wrong" color; it's all a matter of personal preference.

You should use hand quilting needles that range from size 7 to 10, called "betweens." One rule to remember with needles is that the higher the number, the smaller the needle, so choose accordingly. You will also need a thimble on the finger of the hand that pushes the needle into the quilt, and something on the finger below the quilt that receives the needle: a thimble, a piece of adhesive tape, or some other finger protector to keep you from getting stuck.

To start quilting, thread the needle with a single length of thread, approximately the length of your arm, knot one end, and pull the threaded needle through the top and batting, then back through the top. Do not pierce the backing fabric yet! After pulling the needle back through the top, give the thread a yank to pull the knot into the batting; push the knot through with your fingernail if necessary. This buries the knot in the batting. You don't want any unsightly knots showing on a hand-quilted beauty!

Now, take short running stitches through all 3 of the layers to quilt, following along the marked lines of your quilting pattern. Try to have 8 to 10 stitches per inch, and always use a thimble to push your needle through the layers. As you continue to quilt, your stitches will naturally get smaller, so don't be discouraged if they're larger when you first begin. When ending a length of thread, take one or two backstitches and pull the thread up through the fabric of the quilt top, clipping the thread near the surface to bury the end in the quilt.

## Machine-Quilting Tips

Machine-quilting techniques can take up a book by themselves, so I will just give you the basics here. If you need more information, there are many wonderful books on machine quilting available.

A walking or even-feed foot is essential for machine quilting. These feet push the top layers of the quilt through the machine at the same rate that the feed dogs under the throat plate push the bottom layer. Without this foot, you will end up with unsightly puckers, because the bottom layer of fabric is pushed through the machine too quickly.

Also helpful are darning or embroidery feet. To use these feet, refer to the owner's manual of your sewing machine. Some machines need to have the feed dogs dropped down out of use when you use these feet; or else you may need to have the feed dogs covered by a metal plate so that they do not make contact with the fabric. Darning and embroidery feet are meant for the free-motion styles of machine quilting, and for highly decorative quilting designs. Learn to use these feet, as the results are incredible! It will take some practice at first, but remember to stitch slowly so that you don't lose control of your work.

As for sewing machine needles, I recommend size 8 to 12. Use a good quality needle, and replace it often. If your machine is skipping stitches or pulling fibers in the fabric, you definitely need a new needle. A new needle can work miracles!

When machine-quilting, it's best to stitch in the ditch along all of the seamlines before beginning the decorative machine quilting in the spaces. This helps keep your quilt layers from shifting. To stitch in the ditch, just run a line of straight stitching in the space where two pieces of fabric meet (called the "ditch"). Use approximately 10 to 12 stitches per inch. I recommend a neutral-colored all-purpose cotton-wrapped polyester thread for machine quilting, one that blends in with the colors of your quilt, or a clear nylon monofilament thread.

# The Patterns

# 1. Swirling Fuchsia

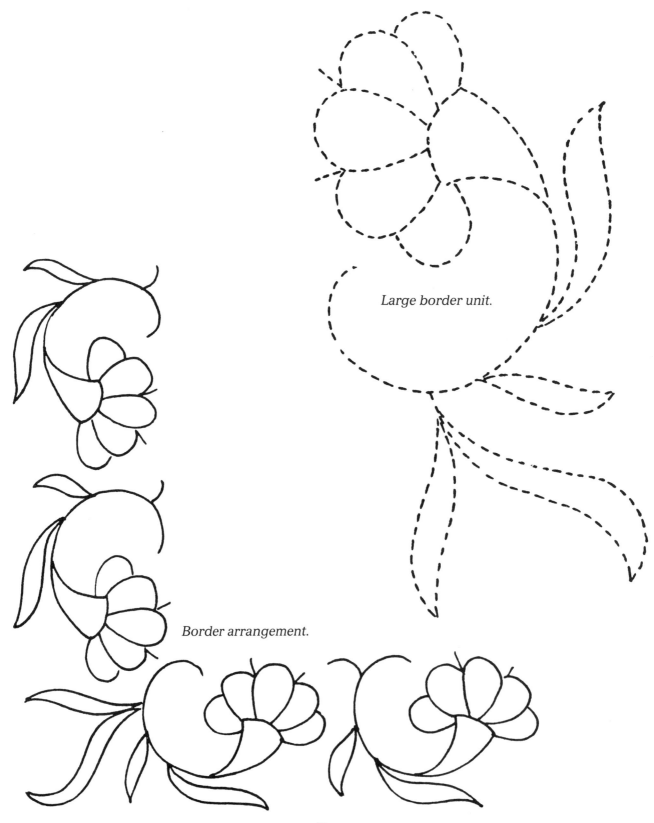

*Large border unit.*

*Border arrangement.*

*Block pattern.*

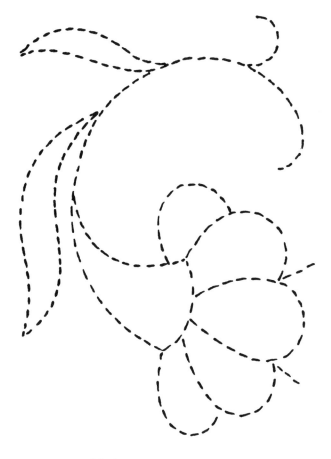

*Medium-sized border unit.*

*Small border units.*

# 2. Moorish Garden

*Block quilting pattern.*

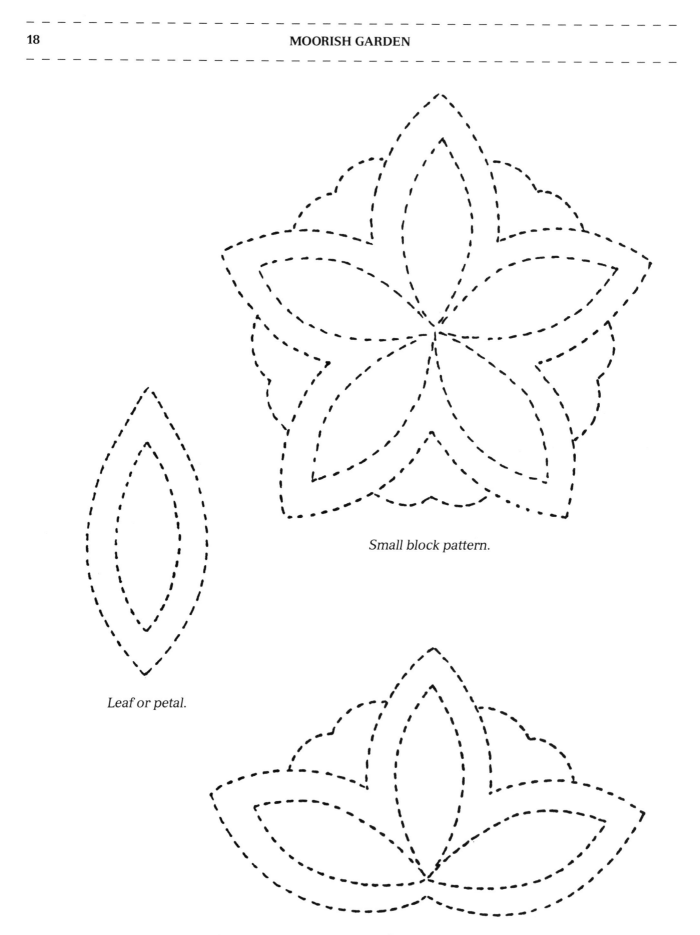

*Small block pattern.*

*Leaf or petal.*

*Corner pattern.*

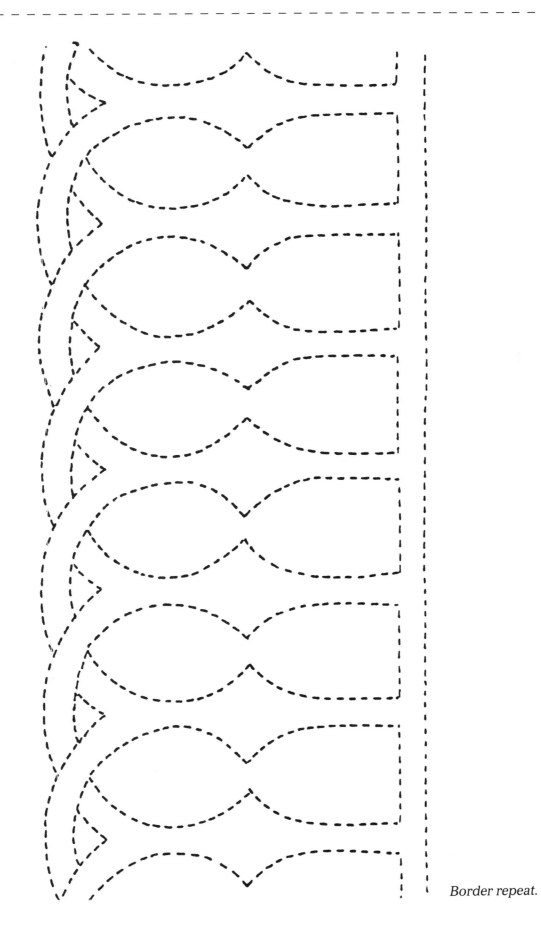

*Border repeat.*

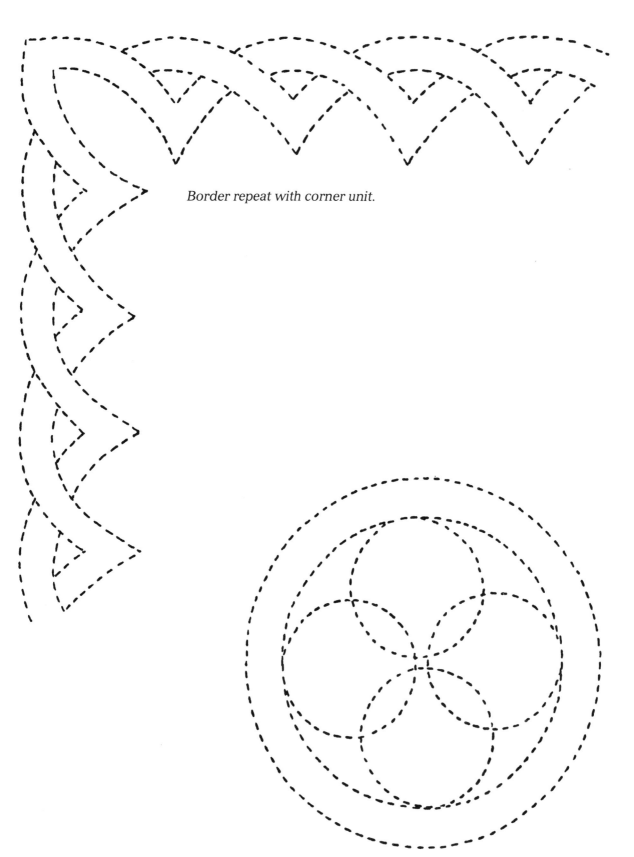

*Border repeat with corner unit.*

*Small block pattern.*

*Border repeat.*

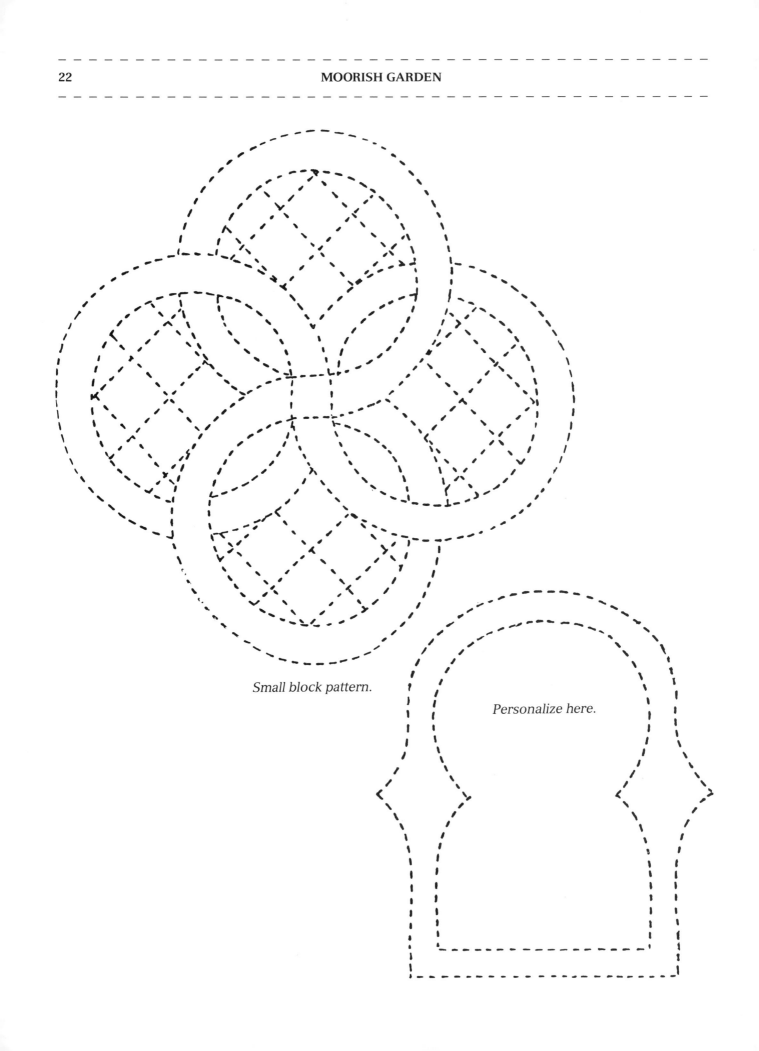

*Small block pattern.*

*Personalize here.*

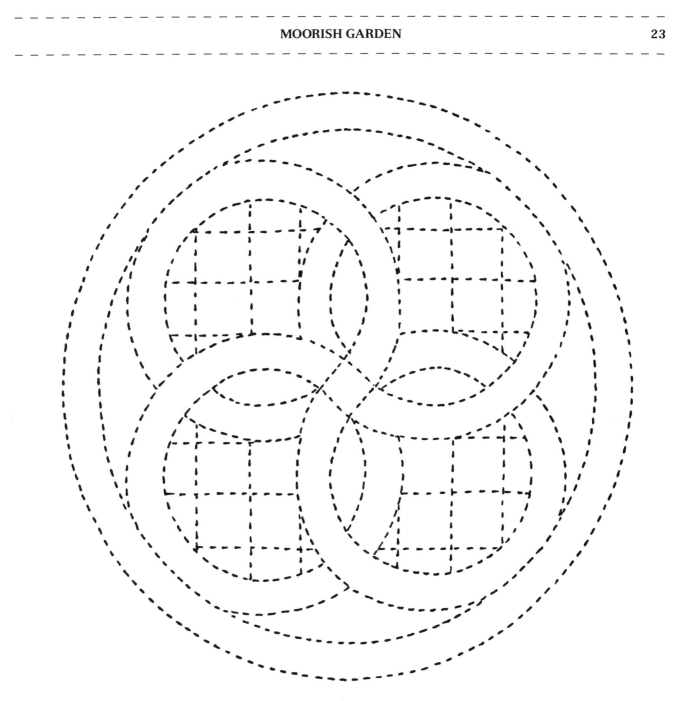

*Block quilting pattern.*

# 3. Palace Gates

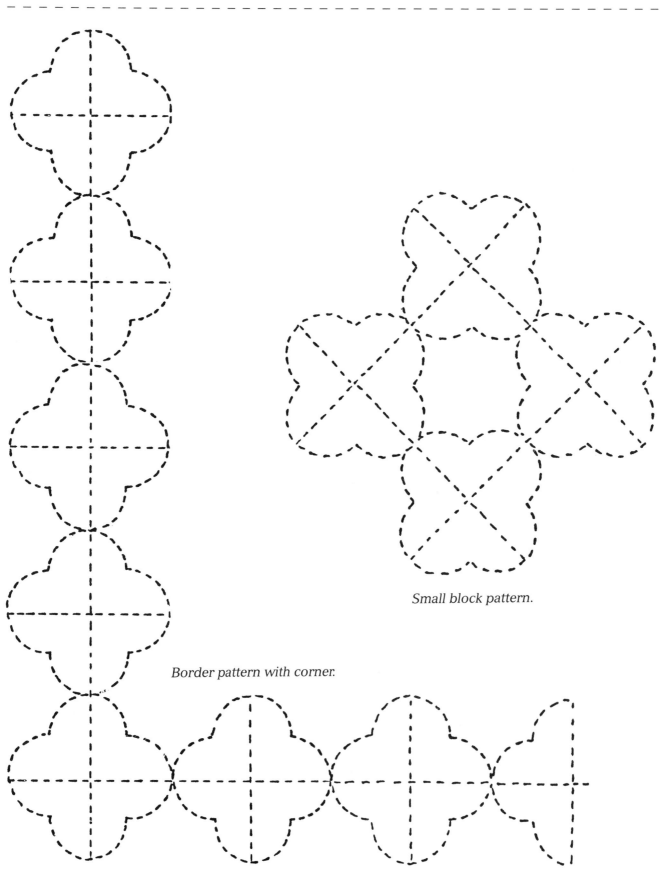

*Small block pattern.*

*Border pattern with corner.*

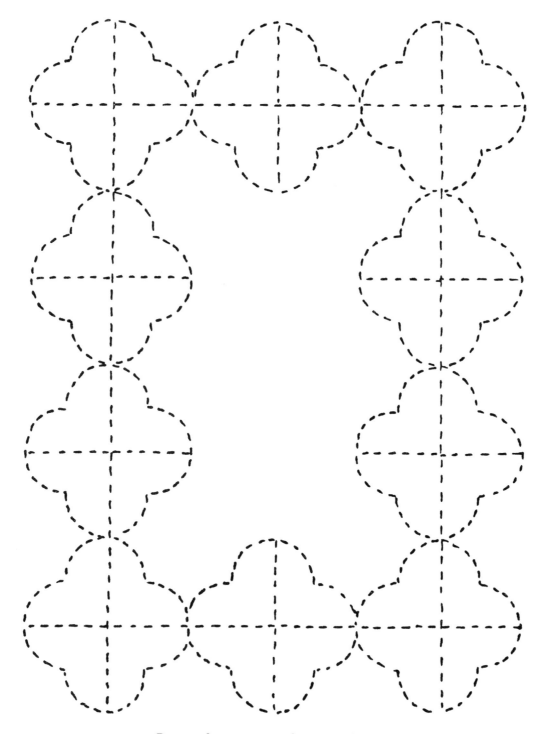

*Pattern for a rectangular area of the quilt.*
*Personalize the center area if you wish.*

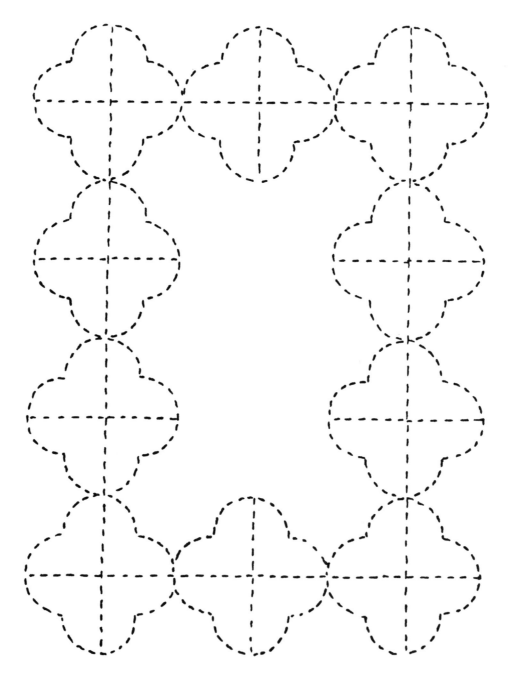

*Rectangular block pattern for a smaller area.*

*Block pattern. May be used as a diamond or a square.*

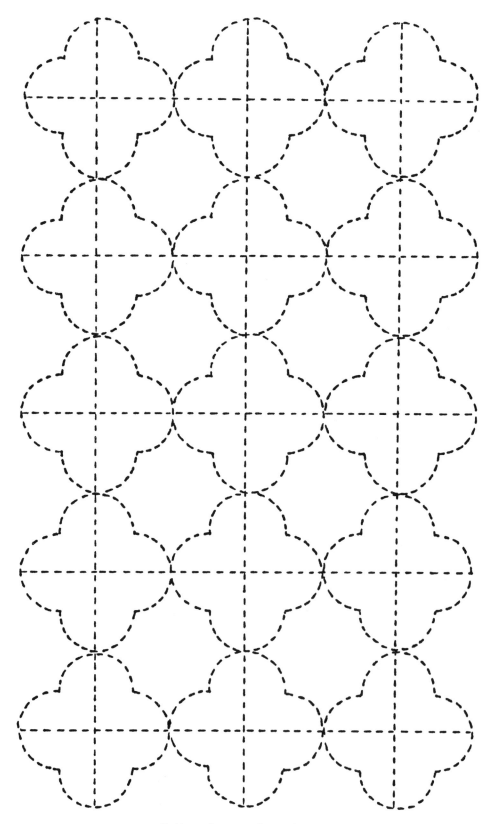

*Pattern for a rectangular area.*

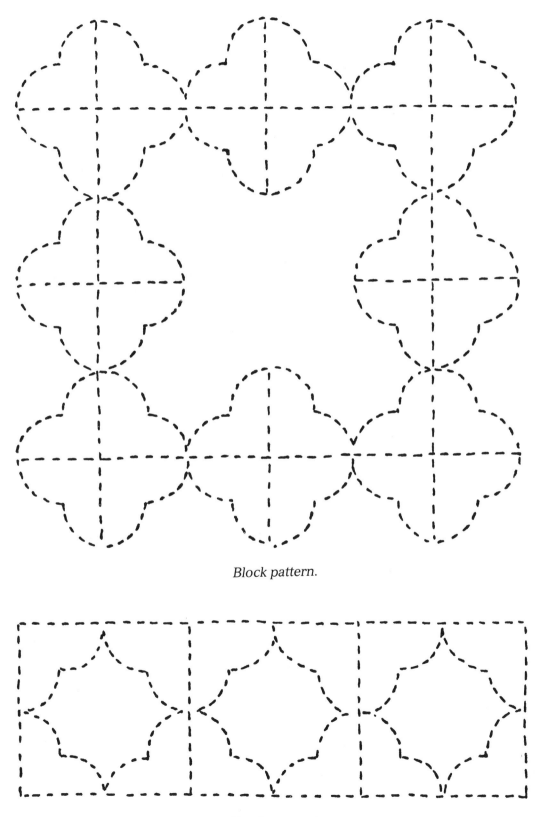

*Block pattern.*

*Border repeat.*

# 4. *Winter Crocus*

*Smaller version of a block pattern.*

*Large pattern.*

centerline

*Half of a block pattern. Use the mirror image for the other side.*

*Small spray.*

*Large spray.*

*Border repeats.*

# 5. Rococo Floral

*Large and small block or border motifs.*

*Border repeat.*

centerline

Half of a large block pattern. Use the mirror image
for the second half.

# 6. Spanish Fans

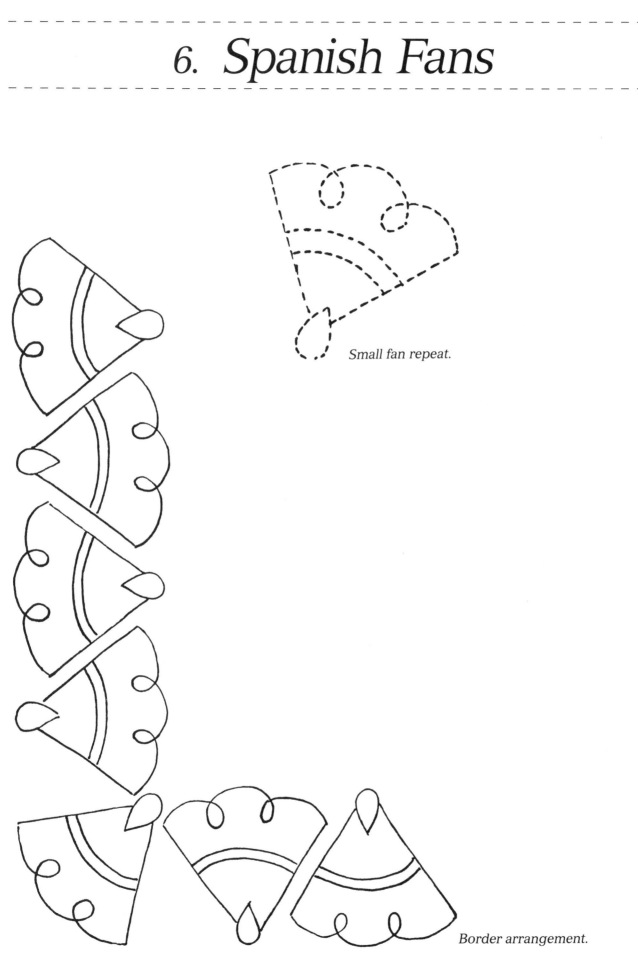

*Small fan repeat.*

*Border arrangement.*

38

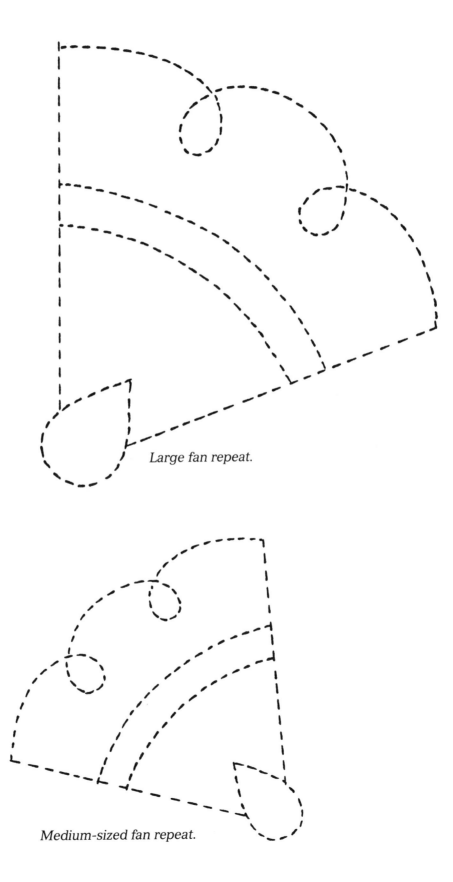

*Large fan repeat.*

*Medium-sized fan repeat.*

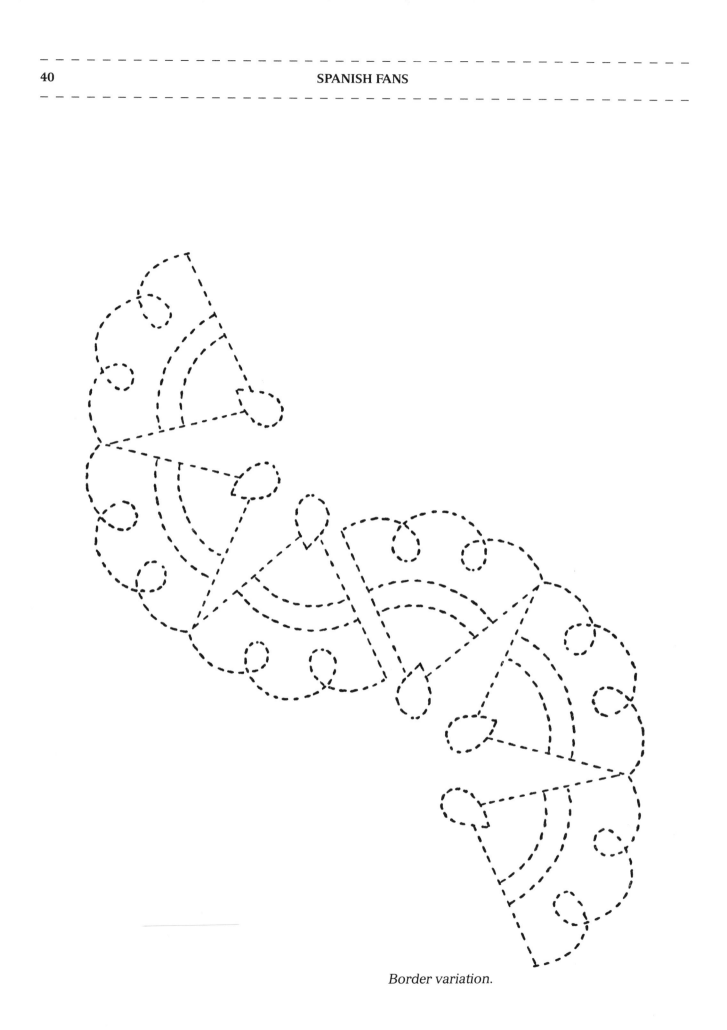

*Border variation.*

*Fan block pattern.*

# 7. Southern Magnolia

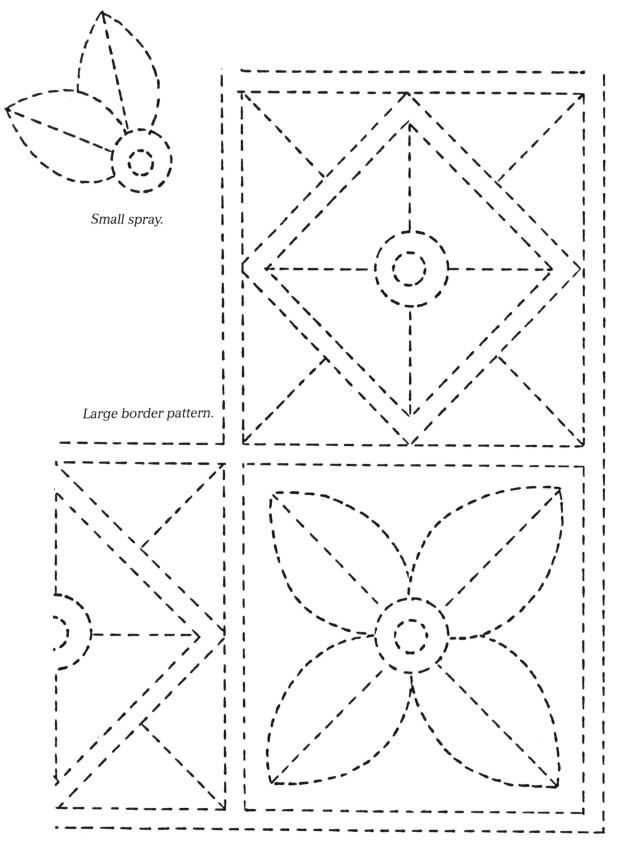

Small spray.

Large border pattern.

*Flower pattern.*

*Block or border pattern. May
be personalized in the center.*

*Large spray.*

*Small border pattern.*

*Block pattern.*

*Large and small flower patterns for blocks or borders.*

# 8. Bridal Garland

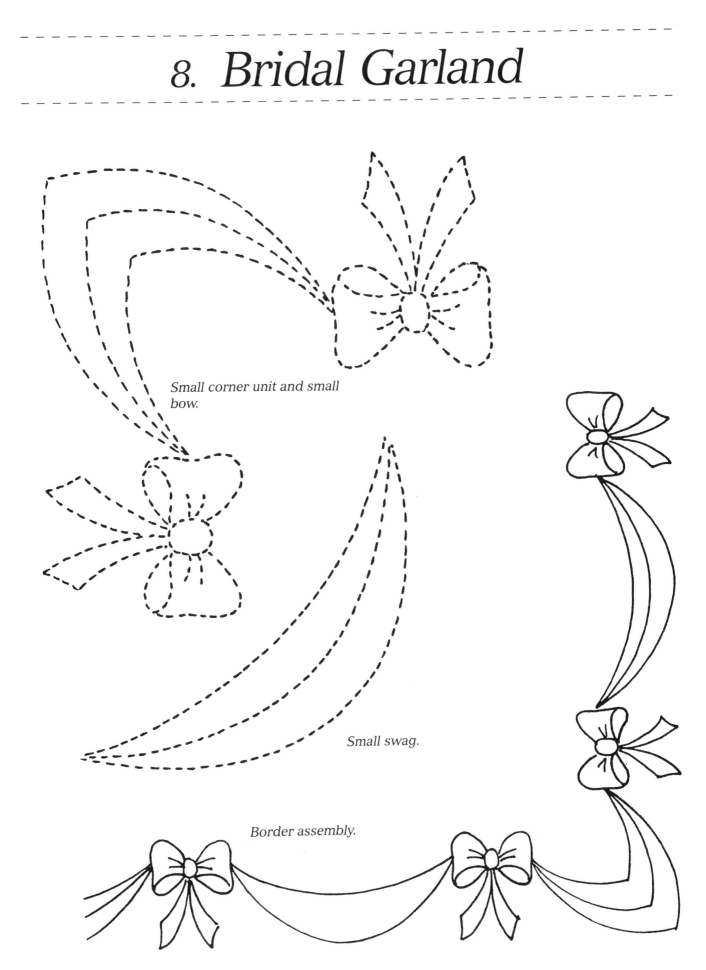

Small corner unit and small bow.

Small swag.

Border assembly.

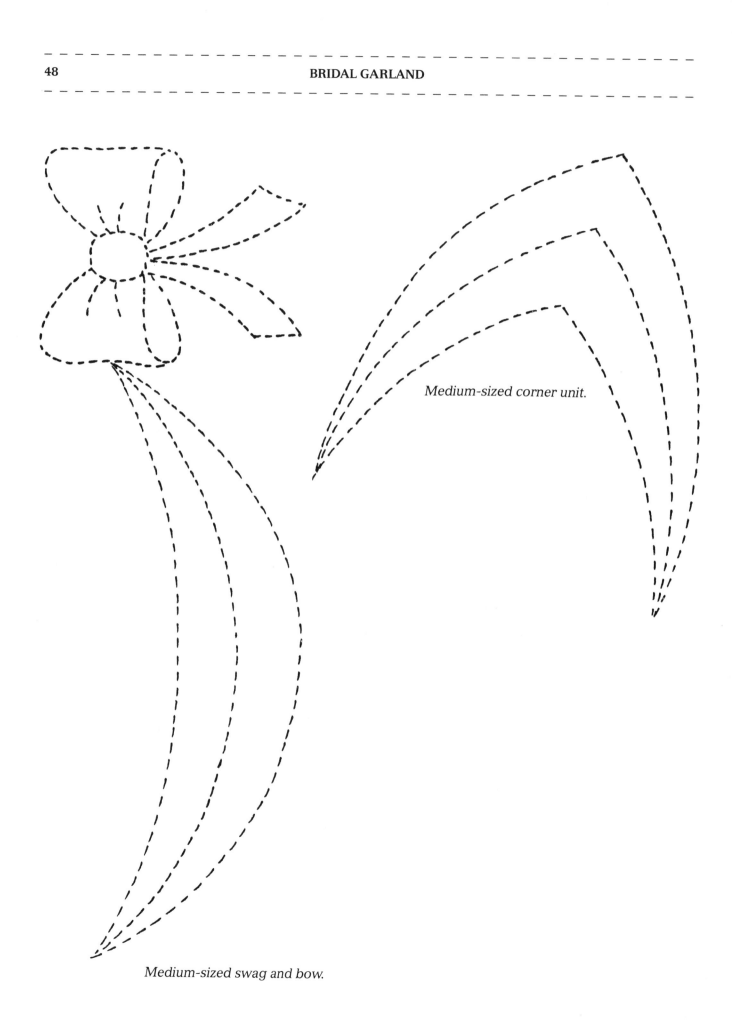

*Medium-sized corner unit.*

*Medium-sized swag and bow.*

*Large bow.*

*Large corner unit.*

centerline

*Half of a block pattern. Use the mirror image for the second half.*

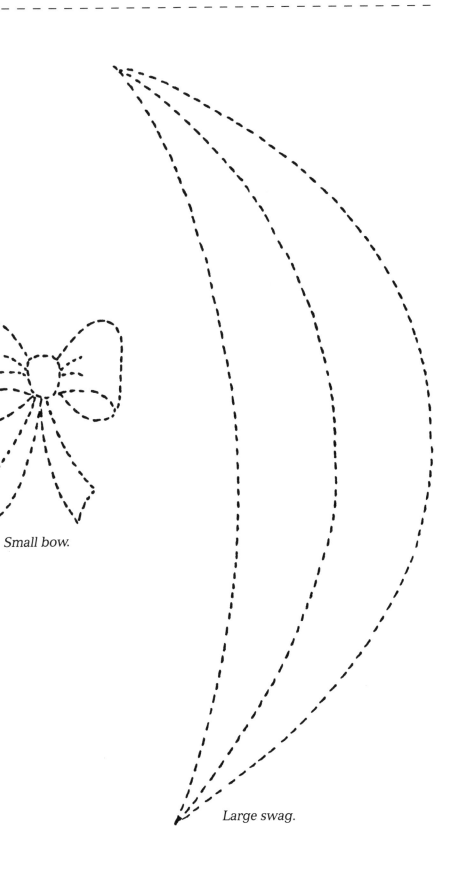

*Small bow.*

*Large swag.*

# 9. Folk Art Flowers

Large flower pattern.

Border assembly.

*Block pattern.*

*Diagram of a border repeat.*

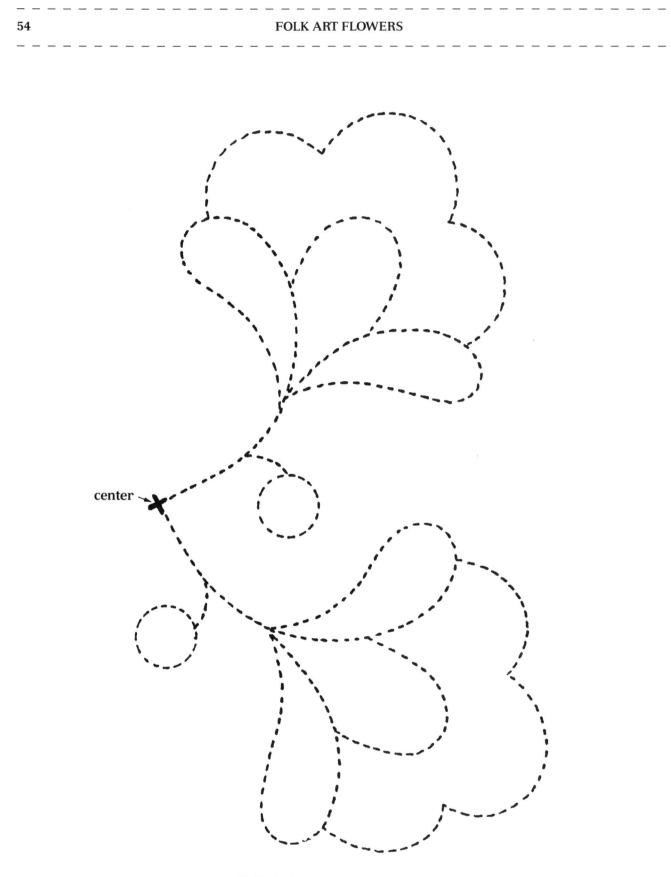

center

*Half of a large block. Use the mirror
image for the second half.*

*Large border repeat.*

*Small border buds.*

*Medium-sized border repeat.*

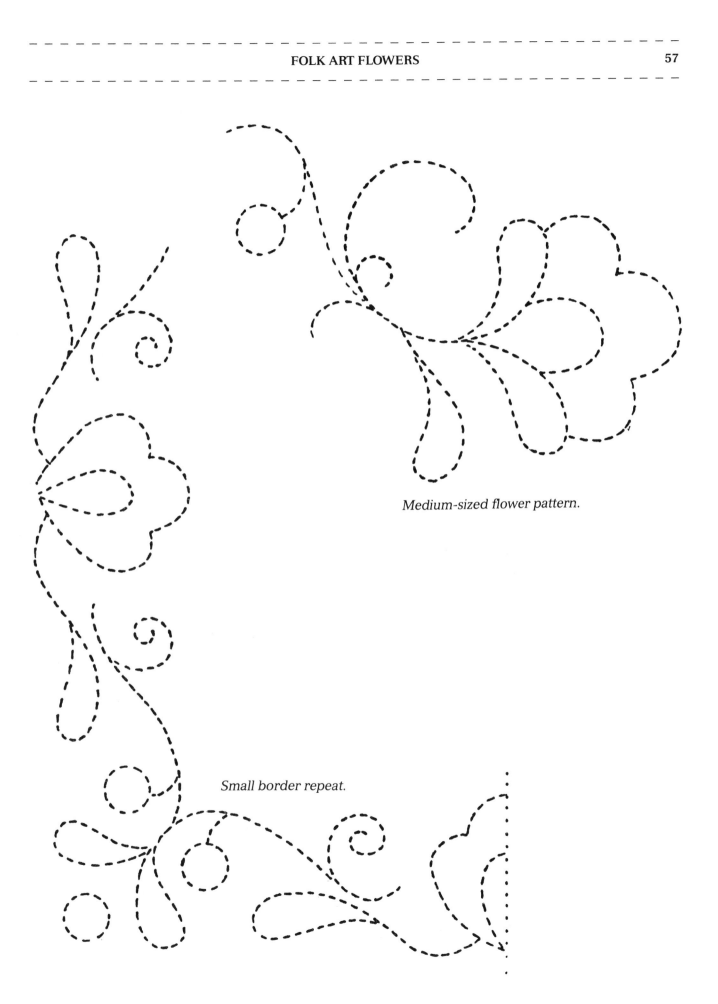

*Medium-sized flower pattern.*

*Small border repeat.*

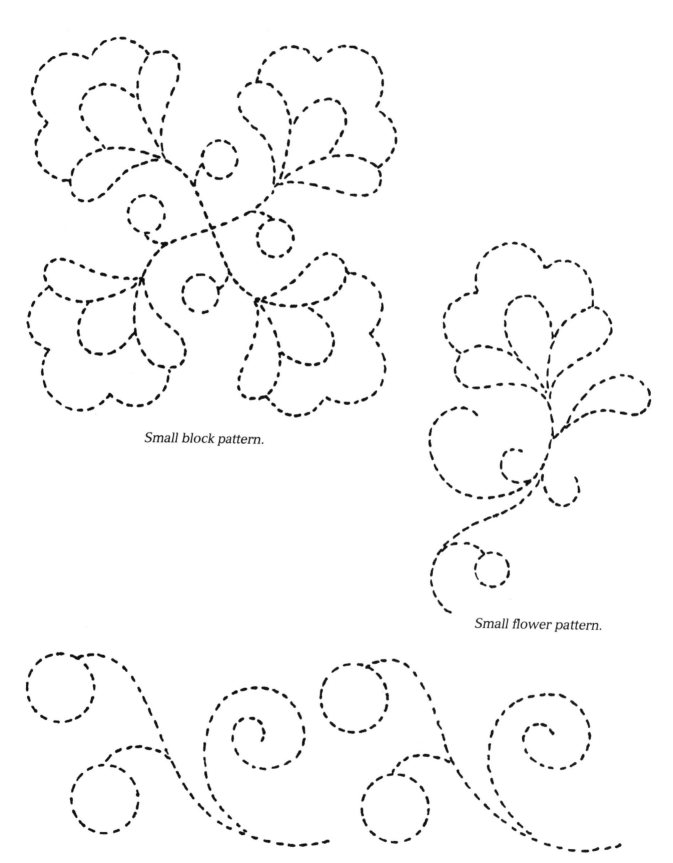

*Small block pattern.*

*Small flower pattern.*

*Large border buds.*

# 10. Art Deco Floral

corner

Border assembly diagram.

Small pattern for block areas.

*Medium-sized border corner.*

*Small border repeat.*

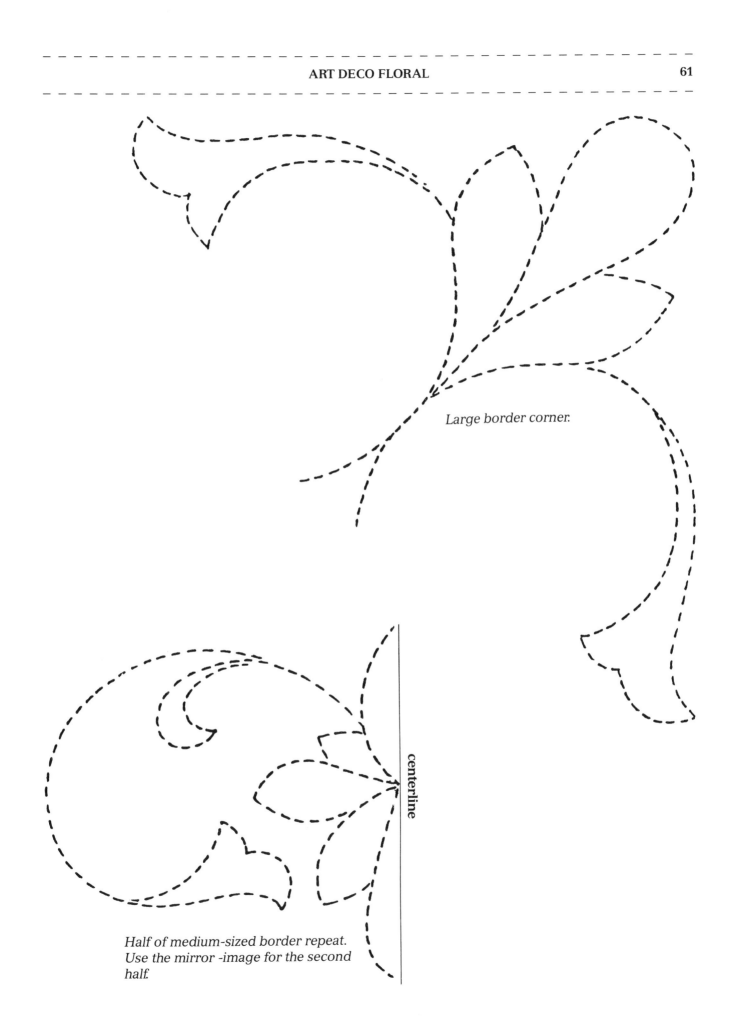

Large border corner.

centerline

Half of medium-sized border repeat. Use the mirror -image for the second half.

*Block pattern.*

*Small spray.*

*Large border repeat.*

# 11. Chain of Flowers

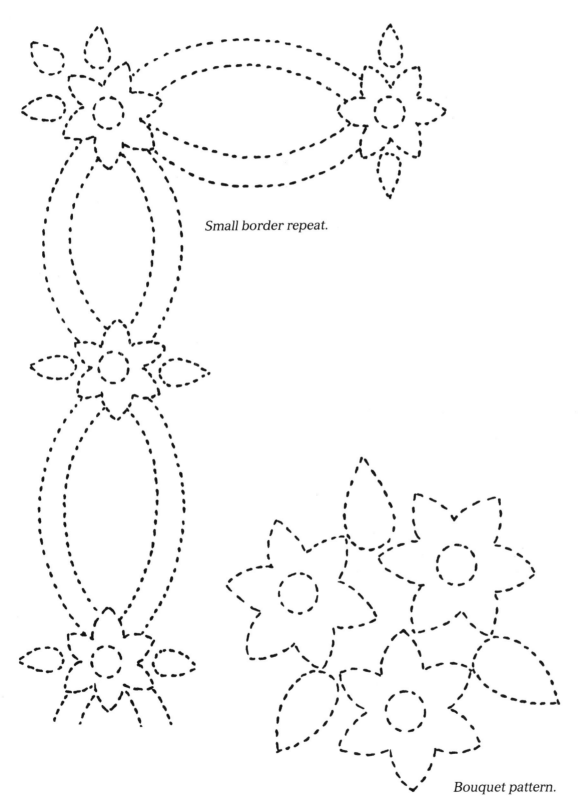

*Small border repeat.*

*Bouquet pattern.*

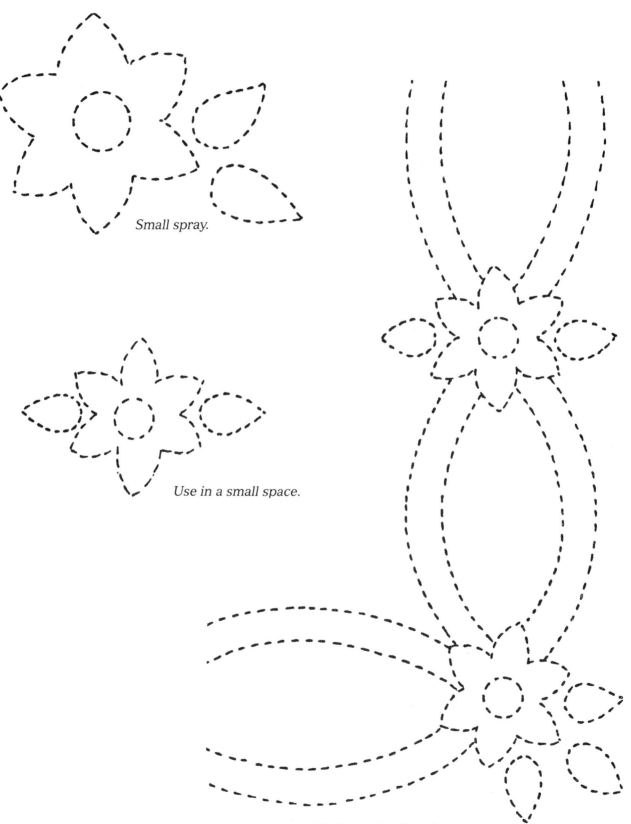

*Small spray.*

*Use in a small space.*

*Medium-sized border repeat.*

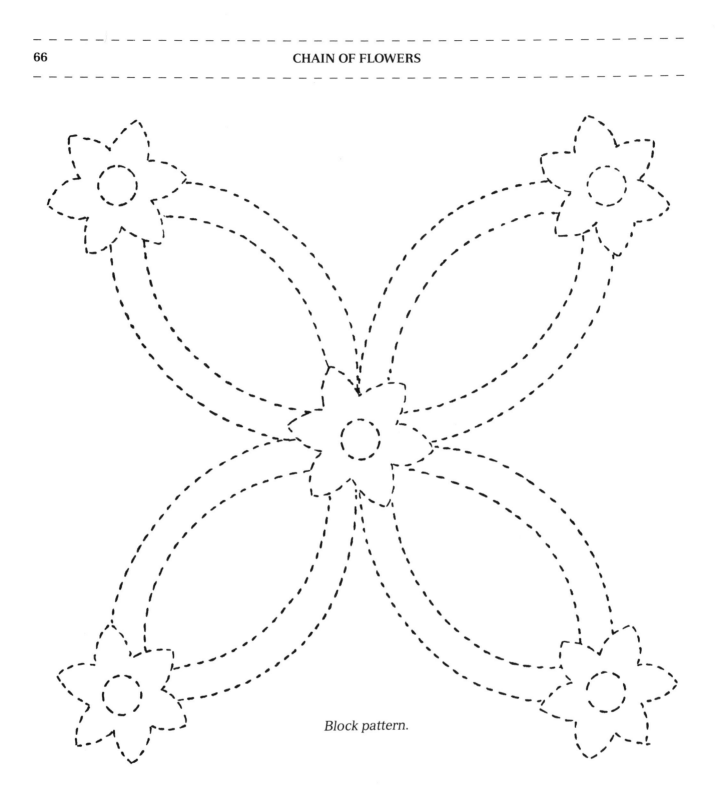

*Block pattern.*

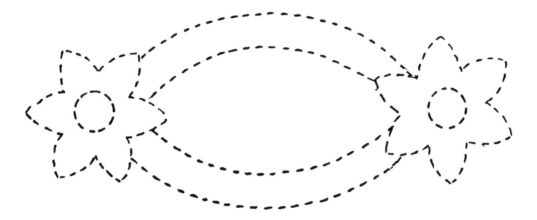

*Personalize in the links of the chain if you wish.*

*Block pattern.*

# 12. *Swirling Hearts*

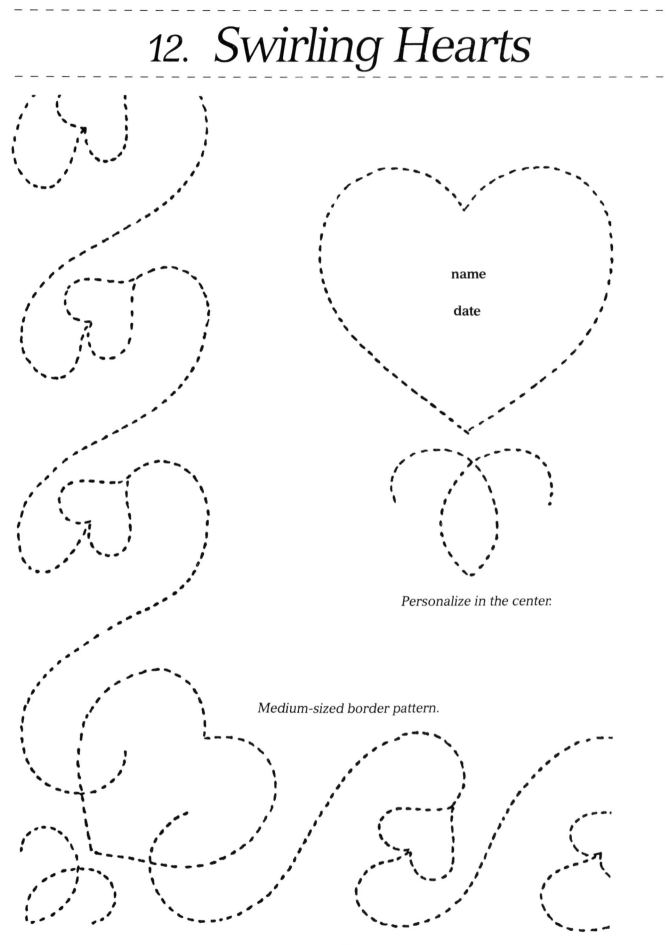

name

date

*Personalize in the center.*

*Medium-sized border pattern.*

*For a small block.*

*Large border pattern.*

*Block pattern.*

*Center unit for a small border.*

Center unit for a large border.

Stacked heart motifs as a border.

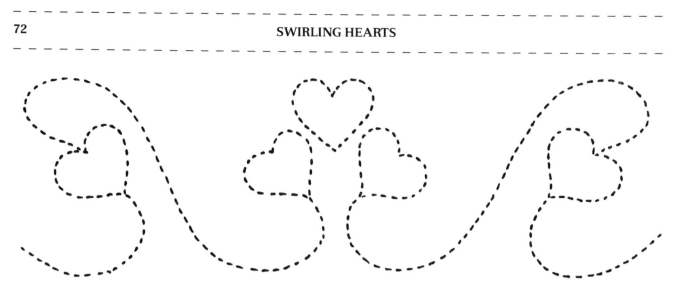

*Center unit for a medium-sized border.*

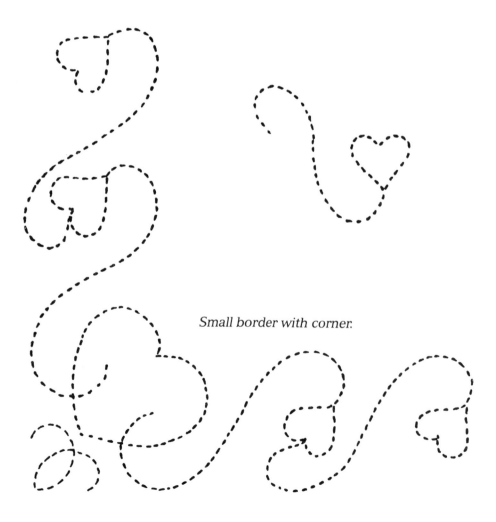

*Small border with corner.*

*Block pattern.*

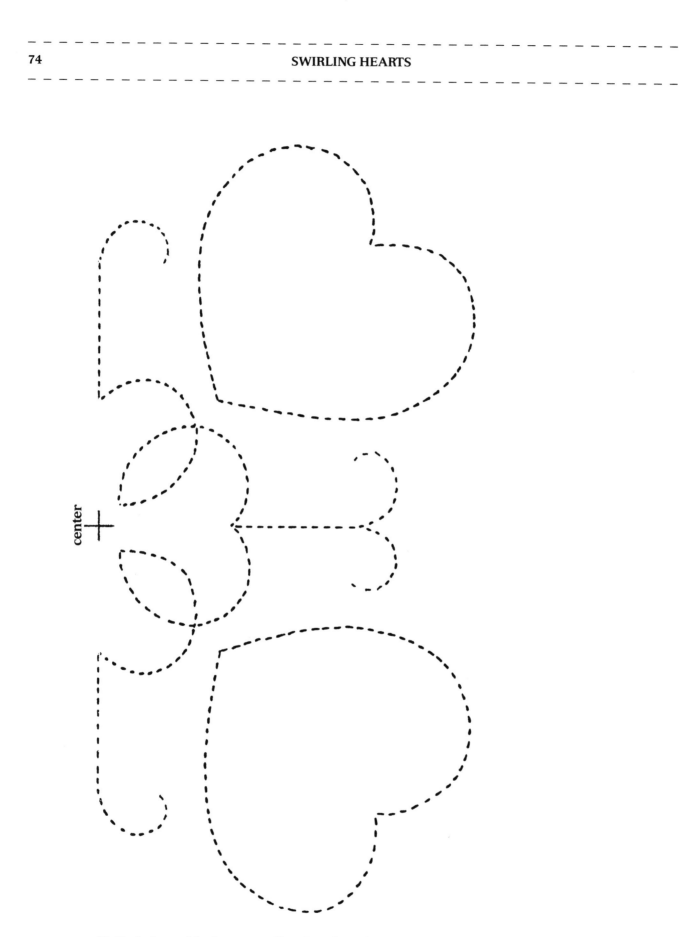

*Half of a large block pattern. Use the mirror image for the second half.*

*Layer the hearts for a border.*

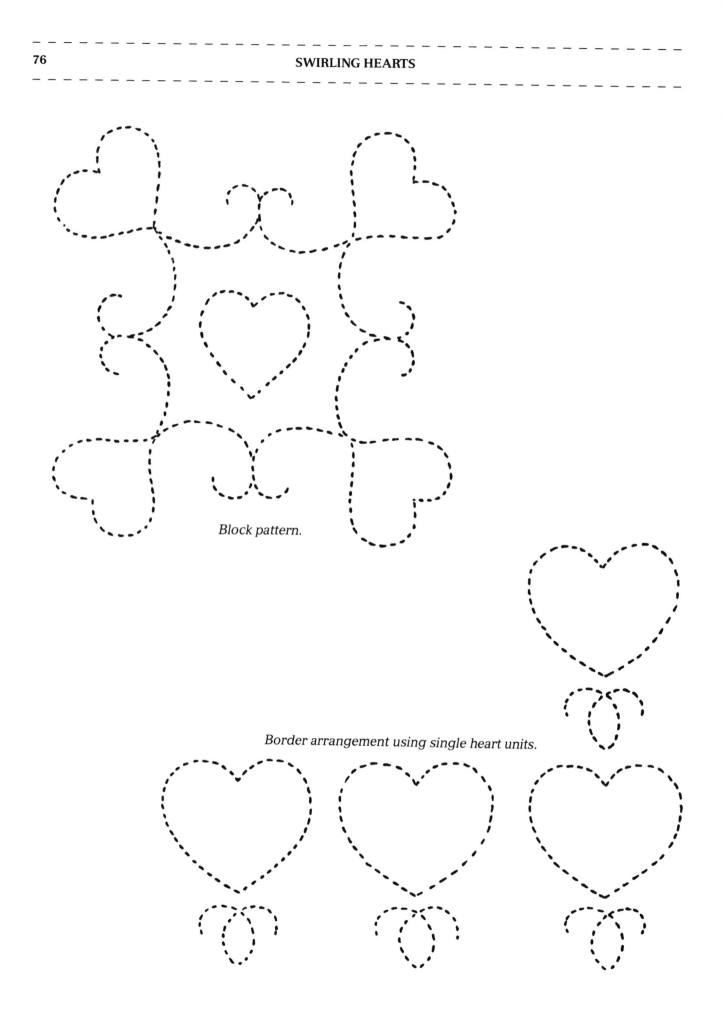

Block pattern.

Border arrangement using single heart units.

# 13. Pick a Posy

*Medium-sized block pattern.*

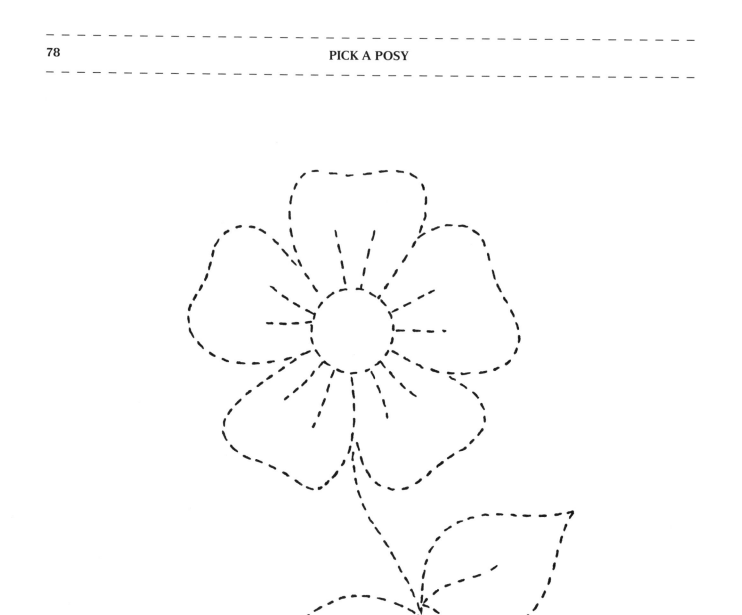

*Large flower with stem.*

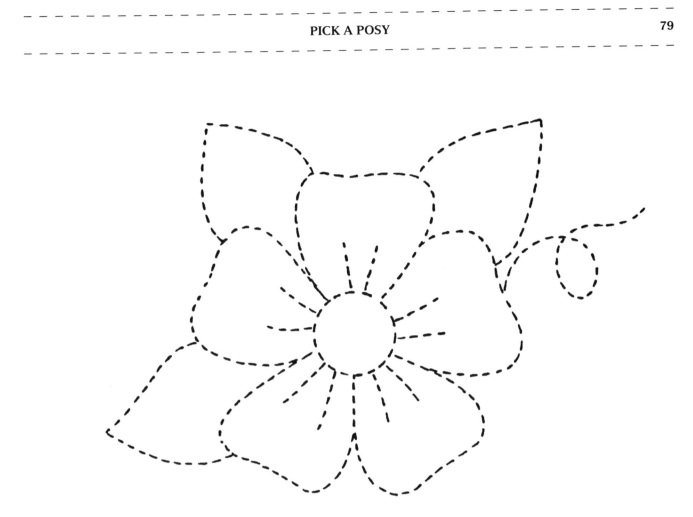

*Large flower pattern.*

*Small flower pattern.*

*Small block pattern. Personalize in the center.*

*Border with corner.*

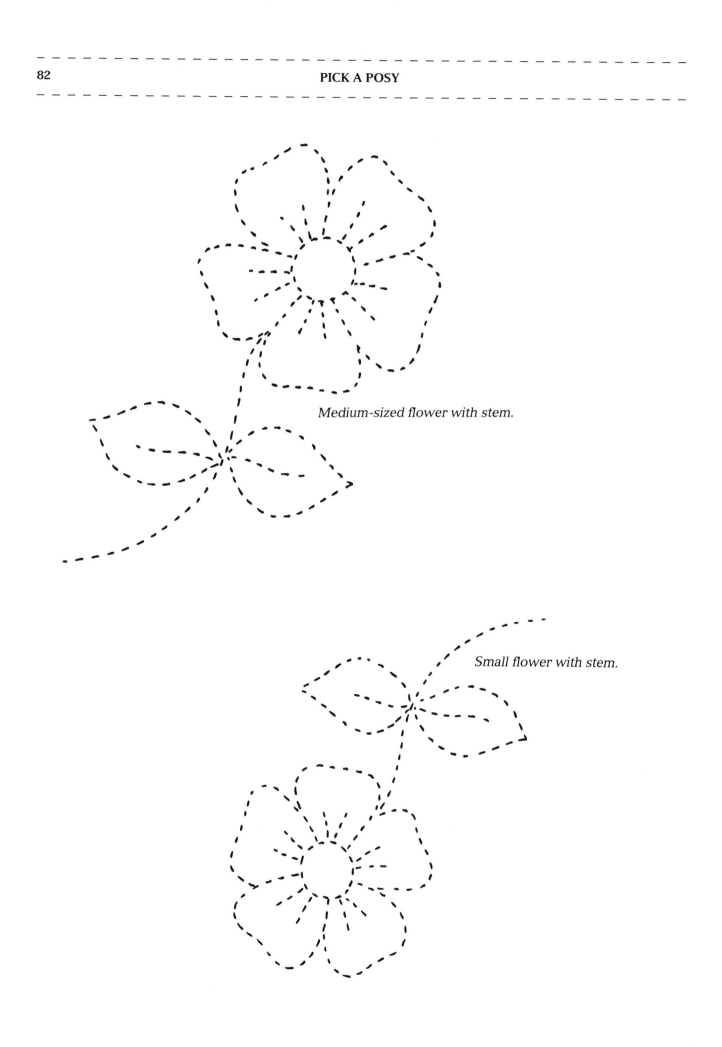

*Medium-sized flower with stem.*

*Small flower with stem.*

*Medium-sized flowers.*

# 14. Bouncing Bunnies

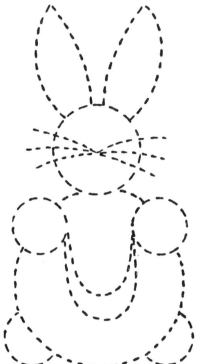

Medium-sized bunny pattern.

The bunny border arrangement.

*Large bunny border.*

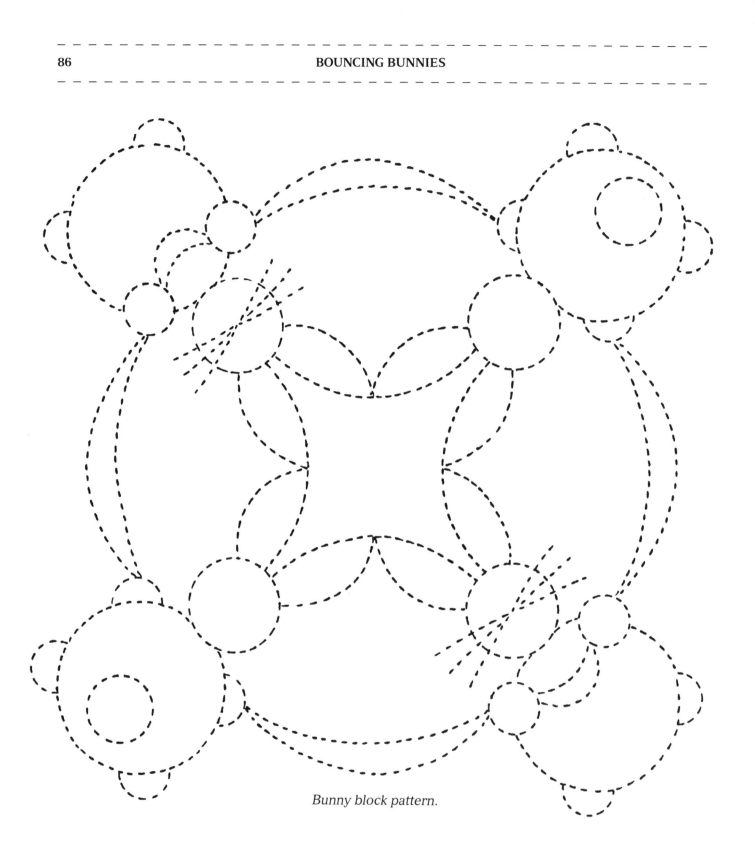

*Bunny block pattern.*

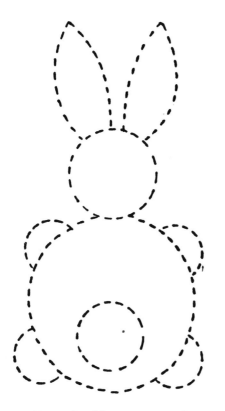

*Medium-sized bunny, rear view.*

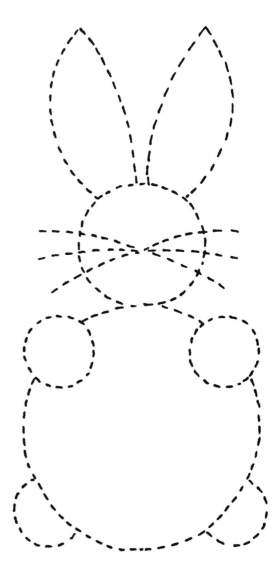

*Large bunny, front view.*

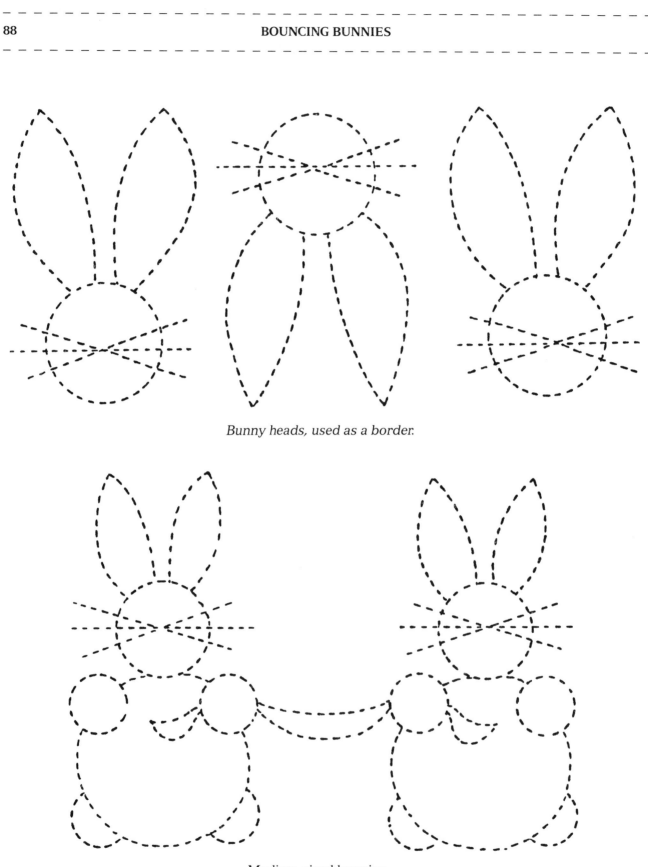

*Bunny heads, used as a border.*

*Medium-sized bunnies.*

# 15. Baby Buggies

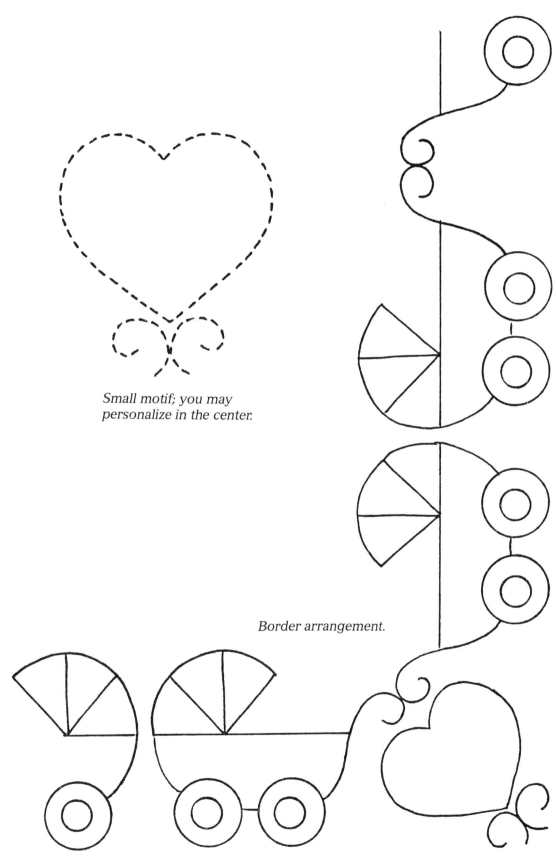

*Small motif; you may personalize in the center.*

*Border arrangement.*

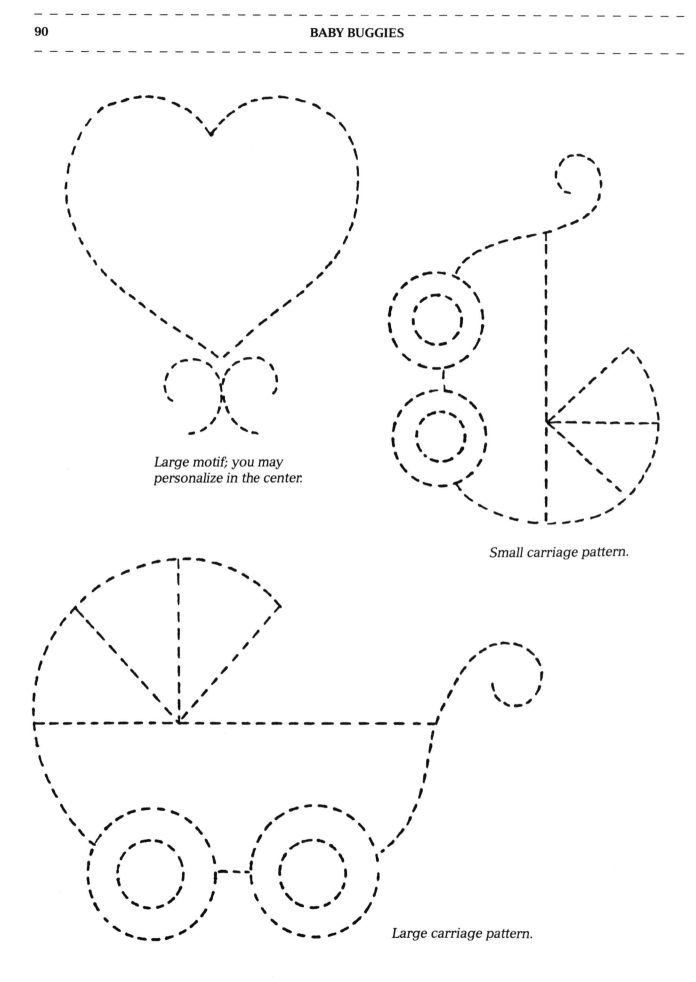

*Large motif; you may personalize in the center.*

*Small carriage pattern.*

*Large carriage pattern.*

# 16. Flutter Byes

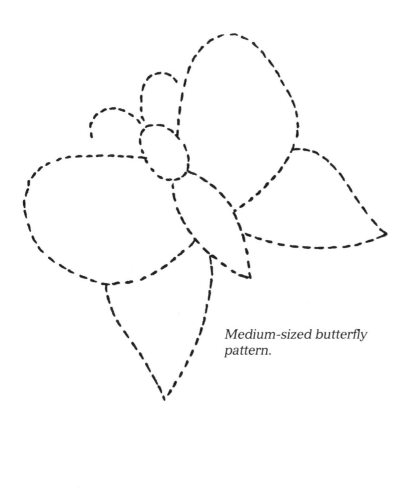

*Medium-sized butterfly pattern.*

*Medium-sized corner unit.*

*Border arrangement with corner unit.*

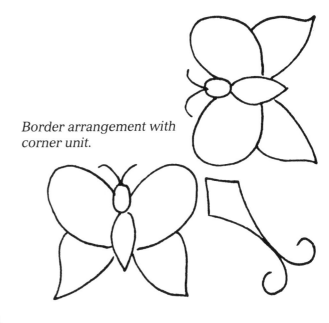

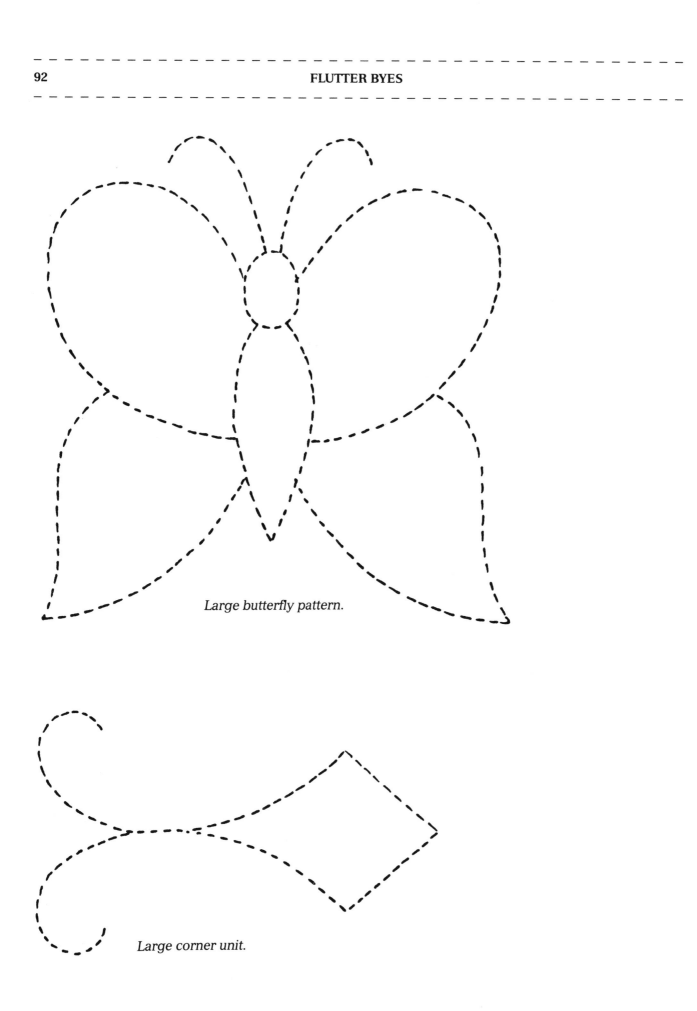

*Large butterfly pattern.*

*Large corner unit.*

*Small butterfly pattern.*

*Small corner unit.*

*Butterflies stacked for a border.*

# 17. Harvest Wheat

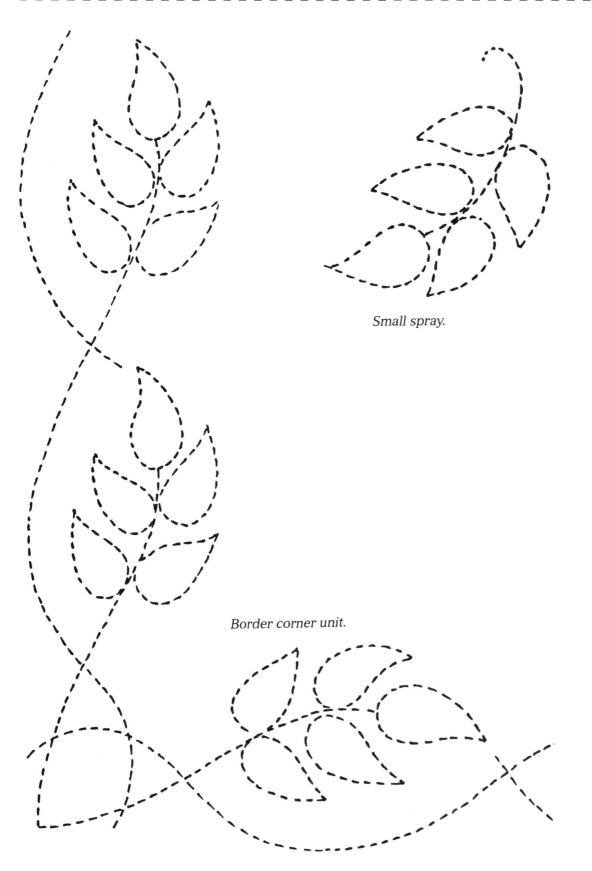

*Small spray.*

*Border corner unit.*

*Large spray.*

*Border assembly.*

*Use this pattern in a triangular area.*

*Block pattern.*

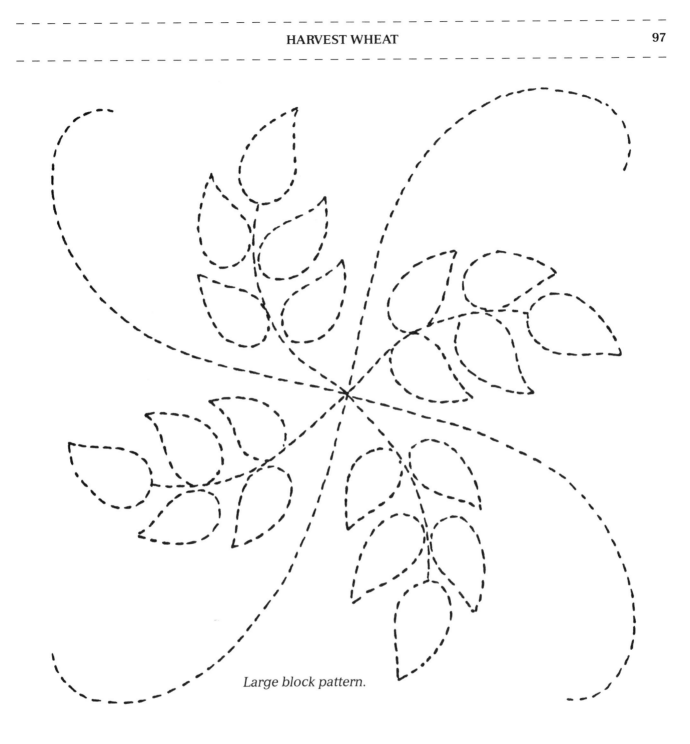

*Large block pattern.*

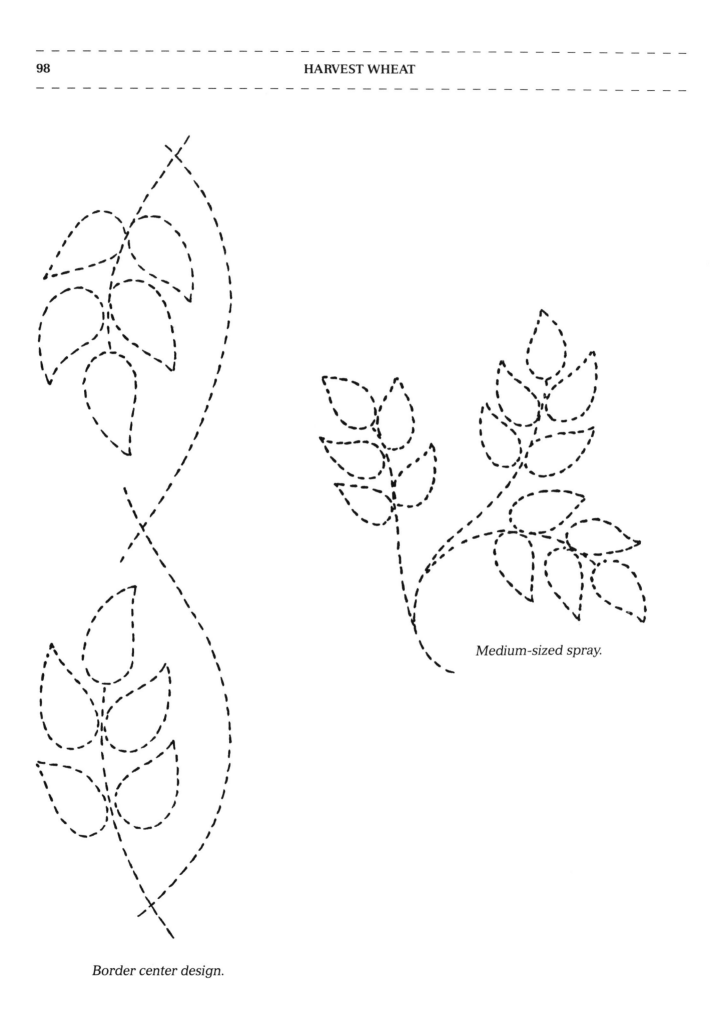

*Medium-sized spray.*

*Border center design.*

# 18. Pine Street

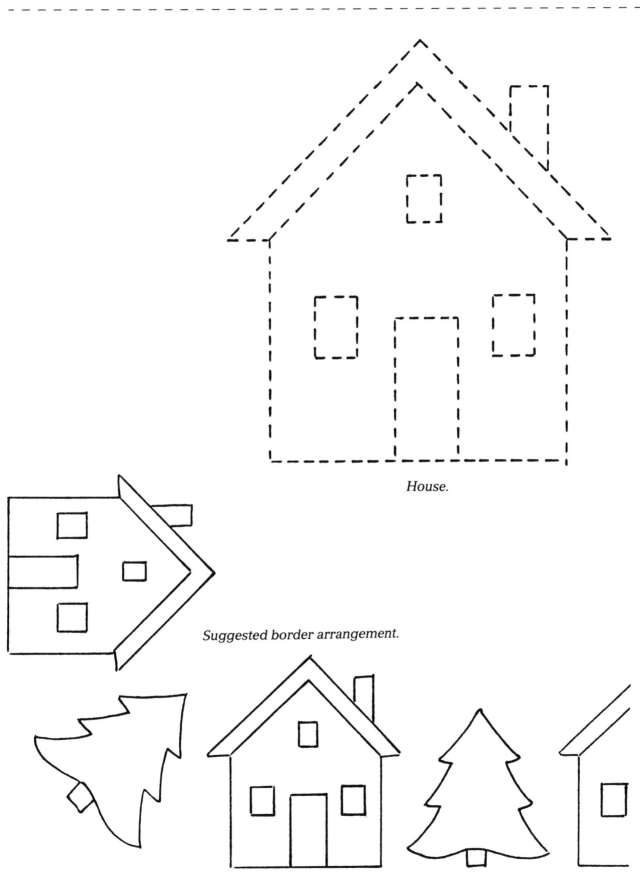

House.

Suggested border arrangement.

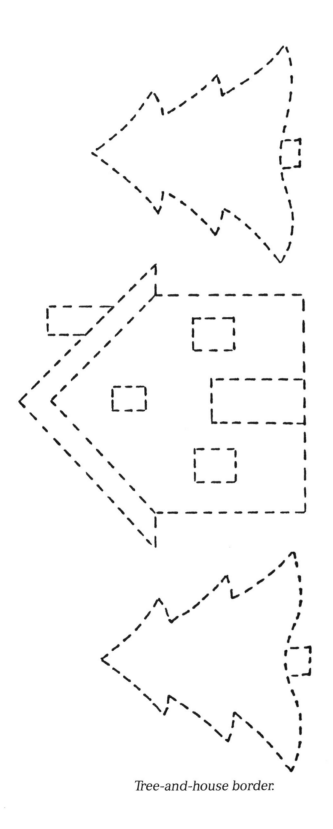

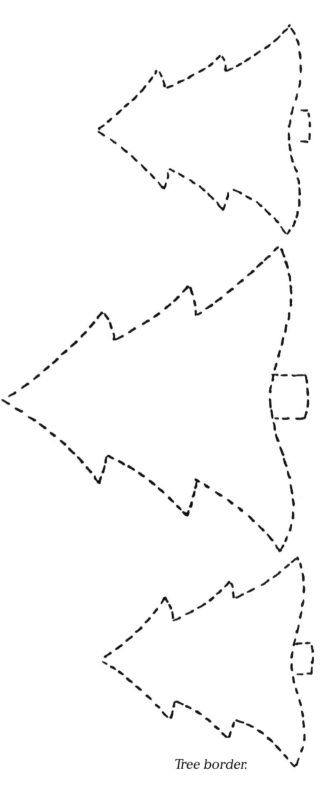

*Tree-and-house border.*

*Tree border.*

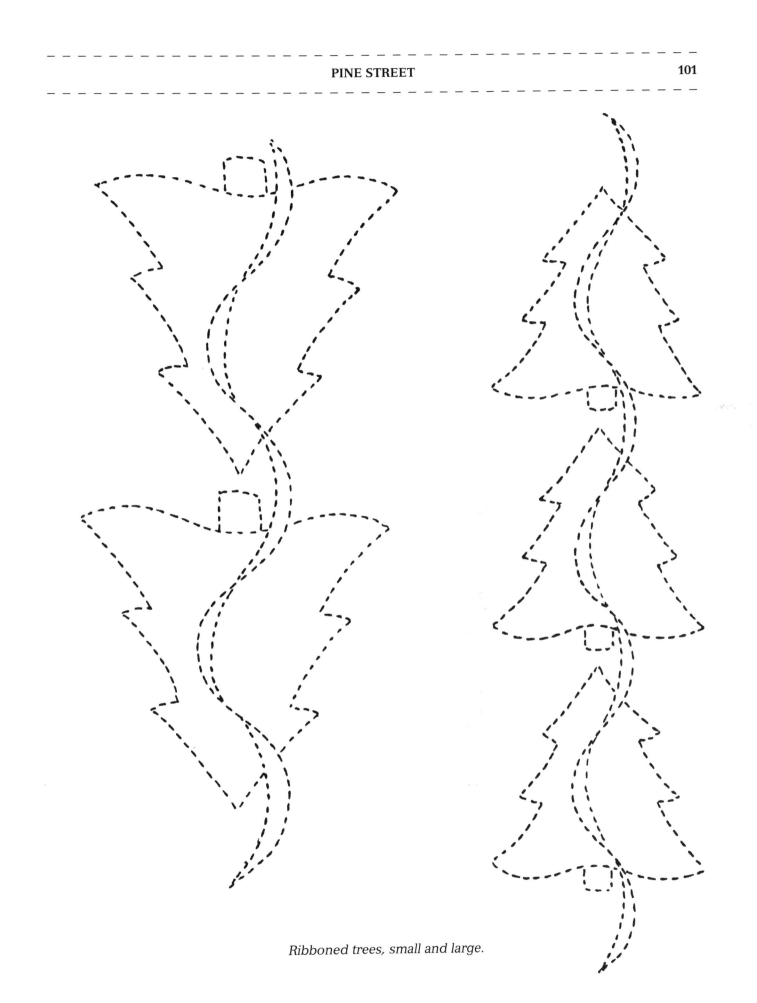

*Ribboned trees, small and large.*

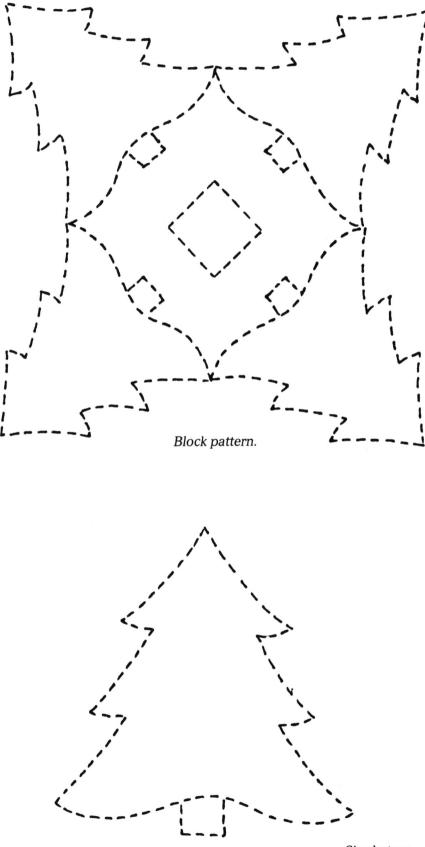

*Block pattern.*

*Single tree.*

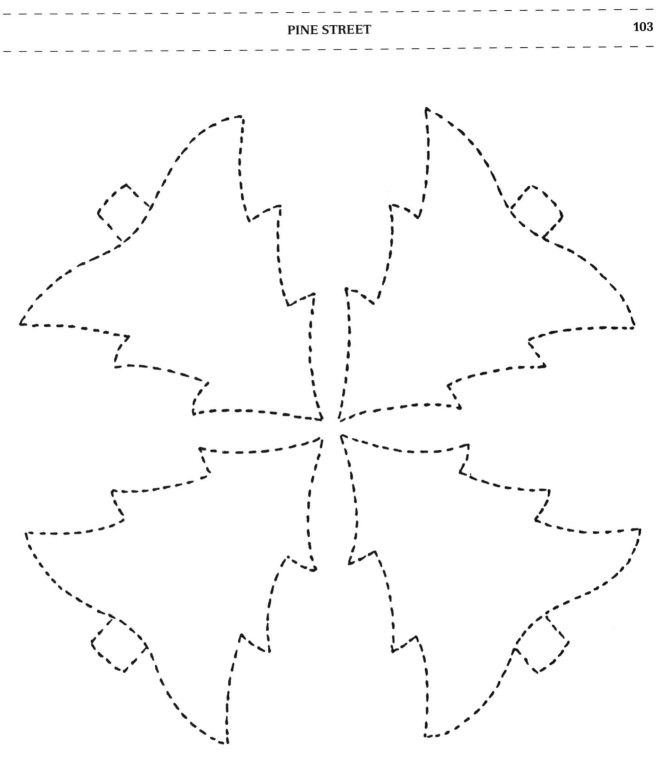

*Large block pattern.*

# 19. Christmas Wreath

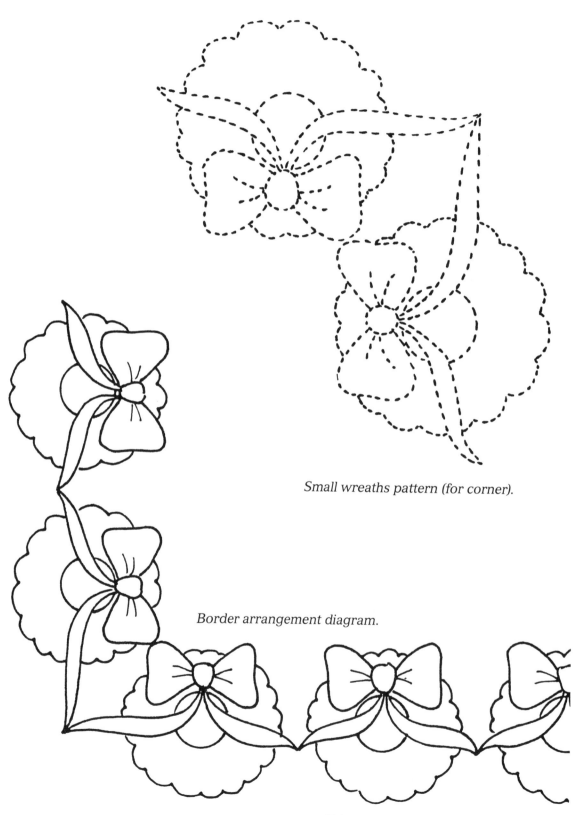

Small wreaths pattern (for corner).

Border arrangement diagram.

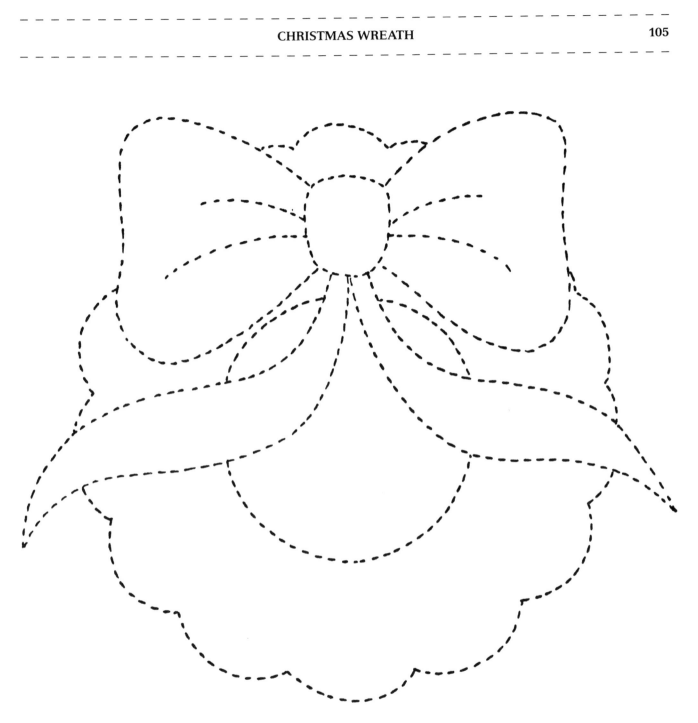

*Large wreath pattern.*

*Small wreath pattern.*

*Medium-sized wreath pattern.*

# 20. Winter Holly

*Large block pattern.*

*Border pattern.*

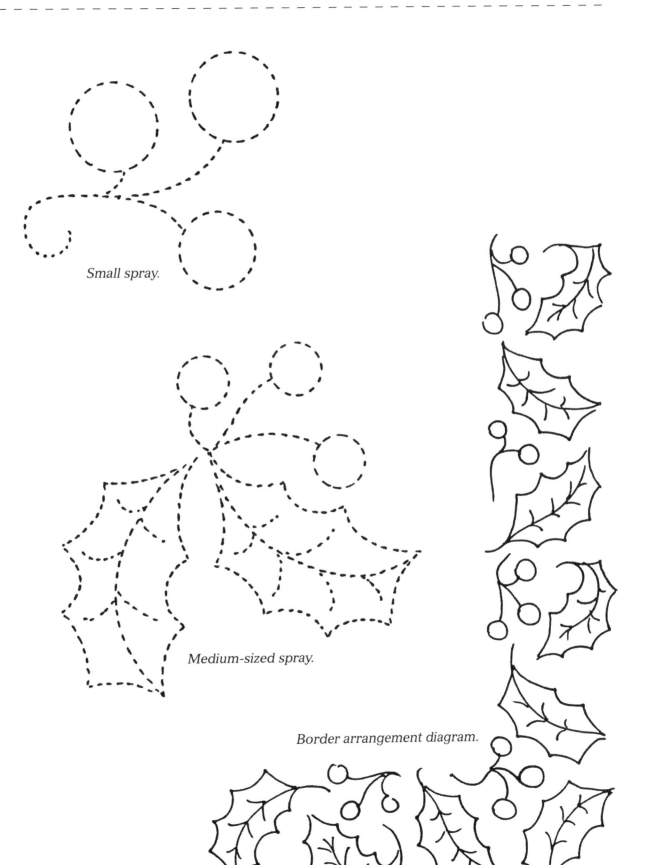

*Small spray.*

*Medium-sized spray.*

*Border arrangement diagram.*

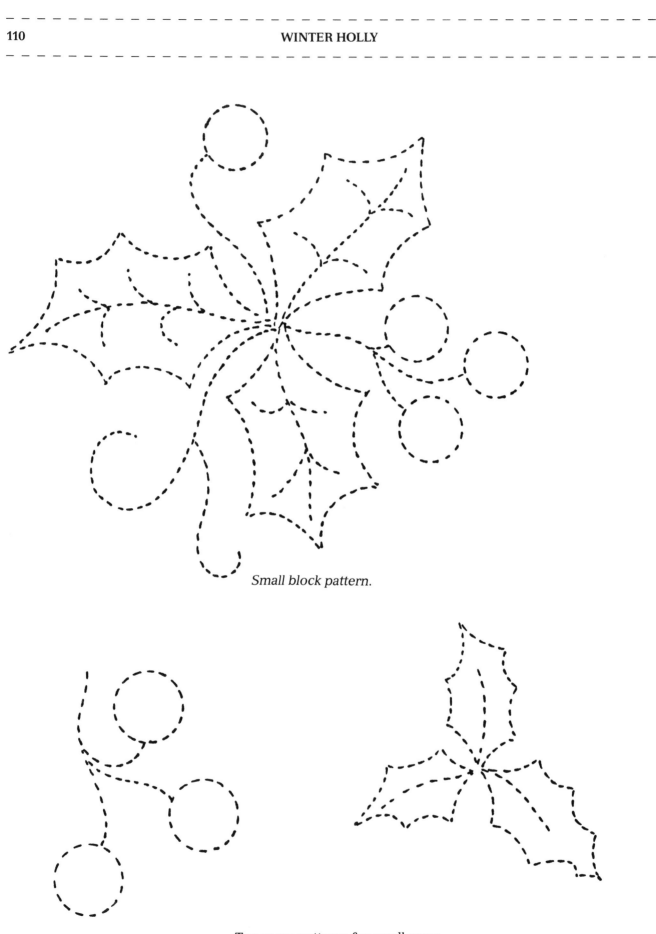

*Small block pattern.*

*Two more patterns for small areas.*

# 21. Northern Lights

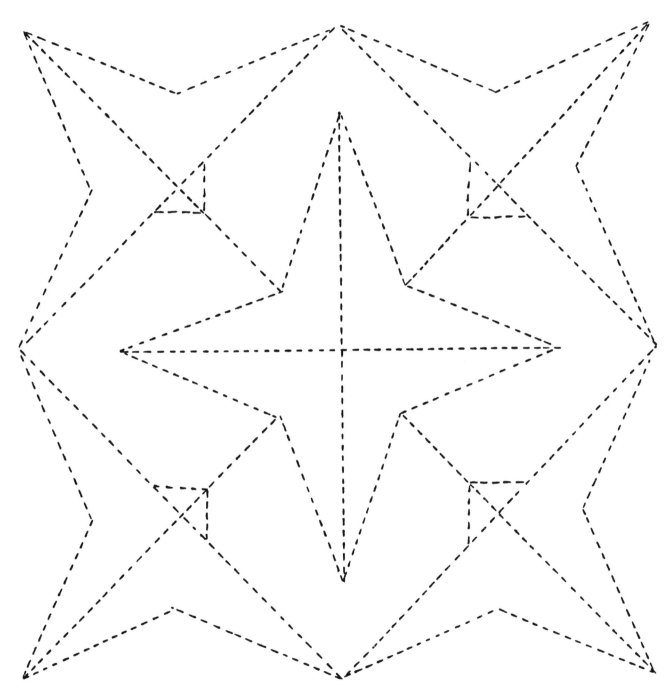

*Large block pattern.*

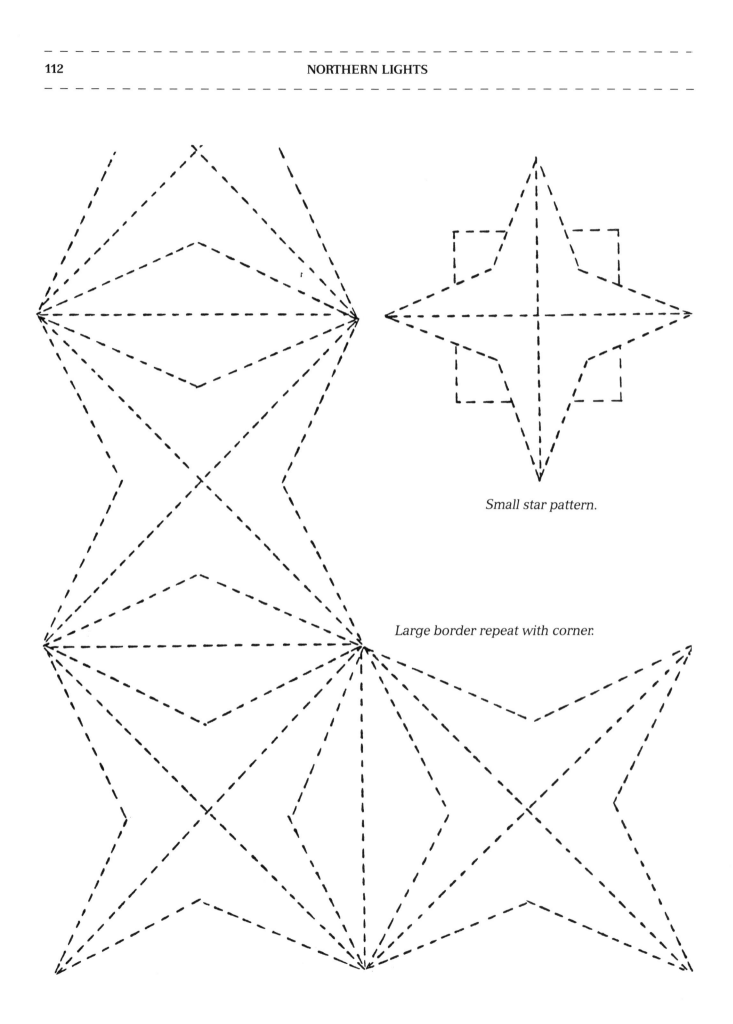

*Small star pattern.*

*Large border repeat with corner.*

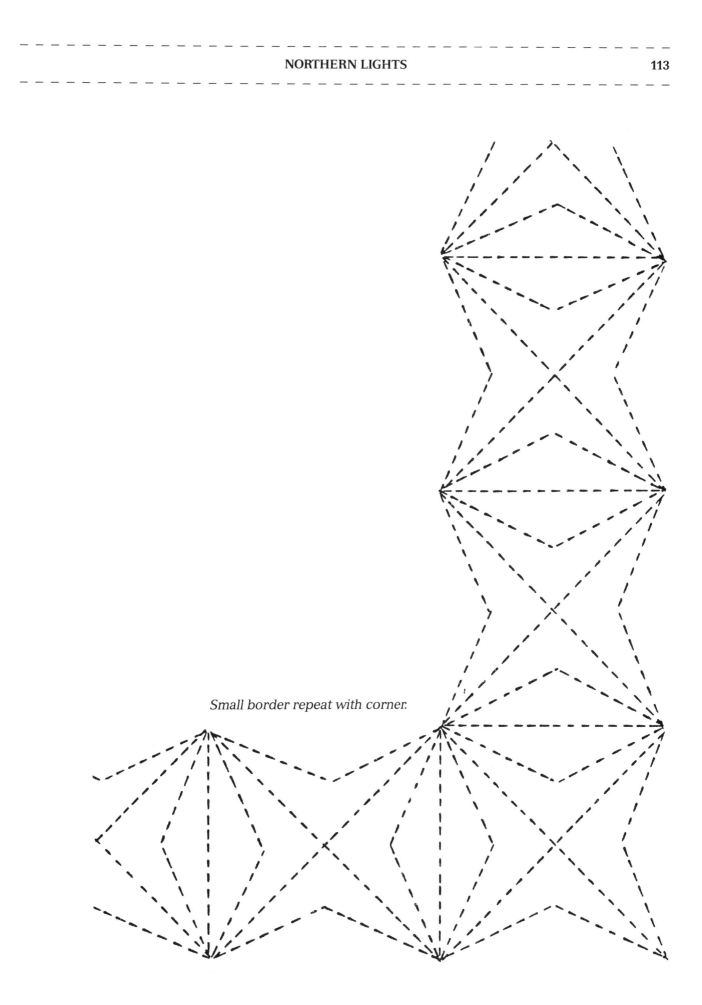

*Small border repeat with corner.*

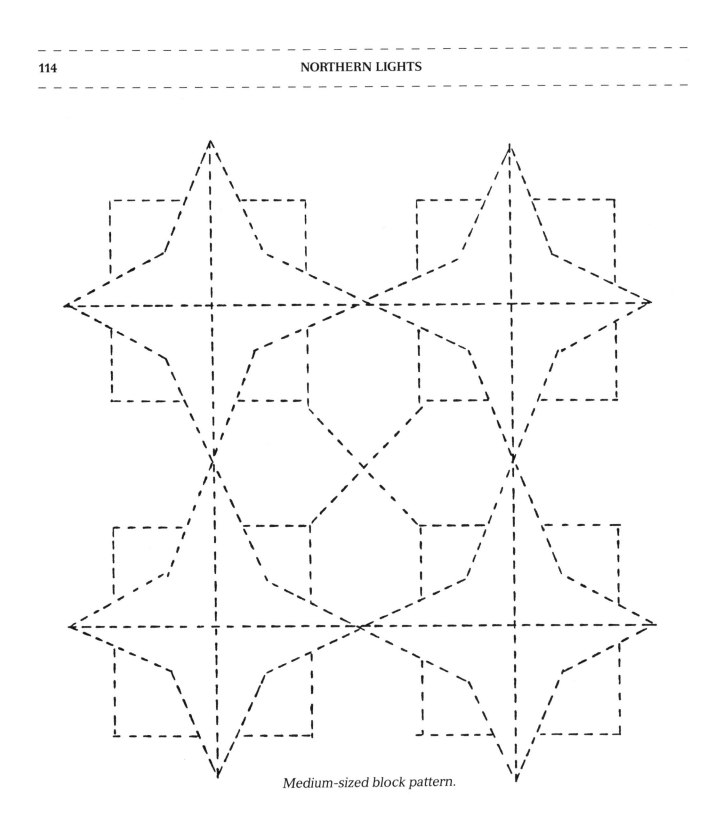

*Medium-sized block pattern.*

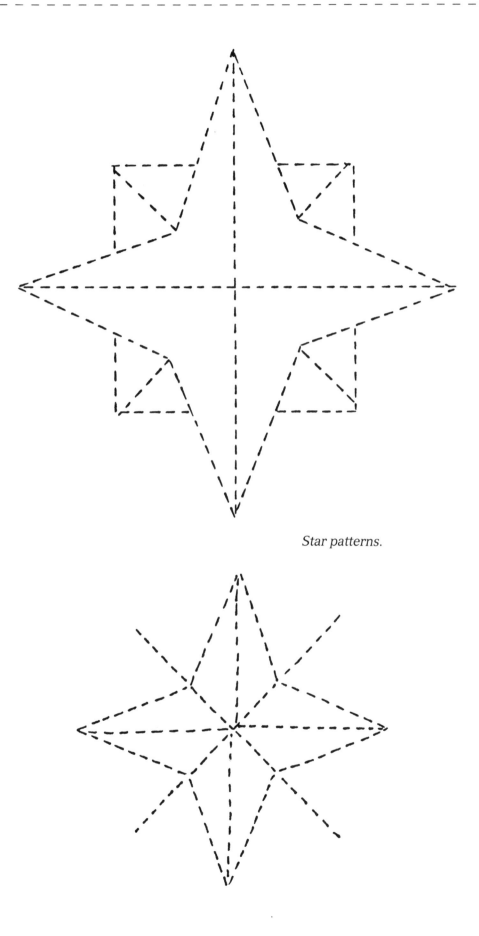

*Star patterns.*

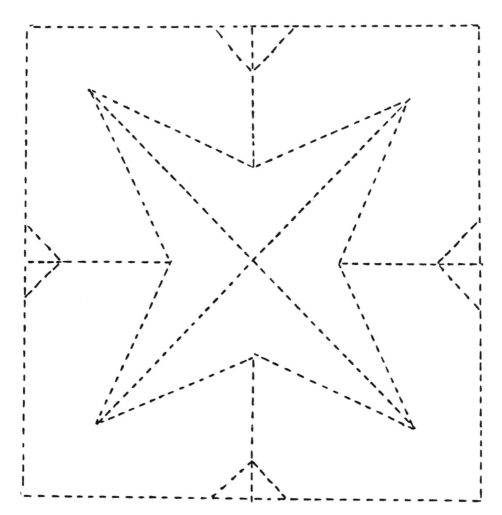

*Use for small block pattern, or stack them for a border.*

# 22. Country Lane

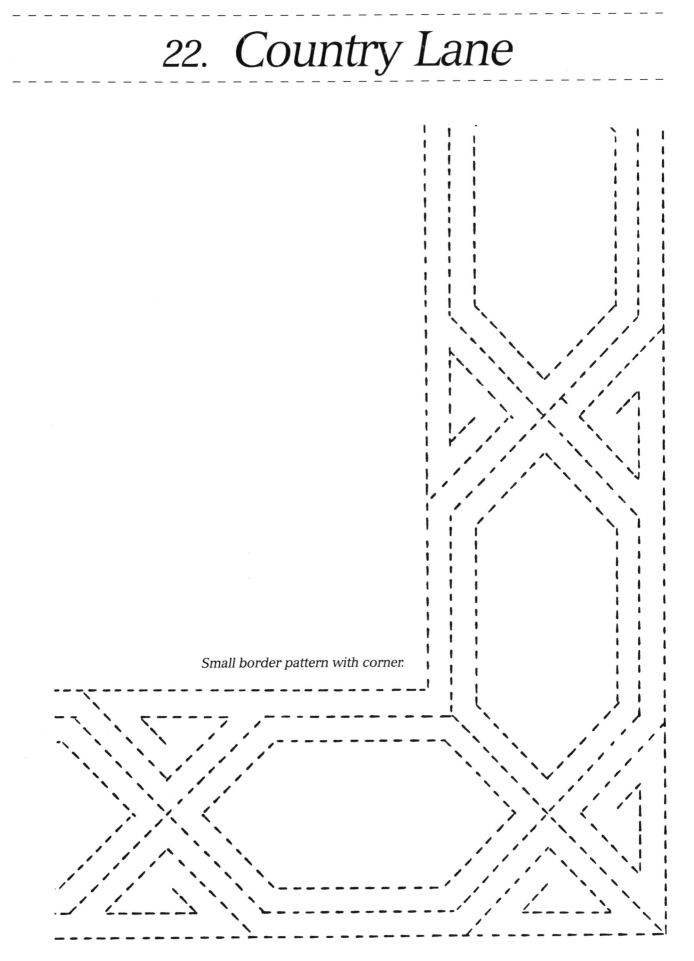

Small border pattern with corner.

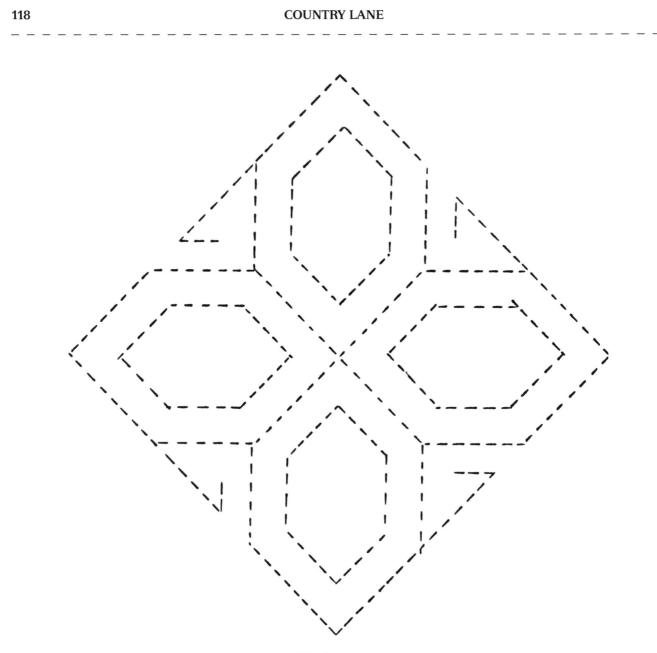

*Block pattern.*

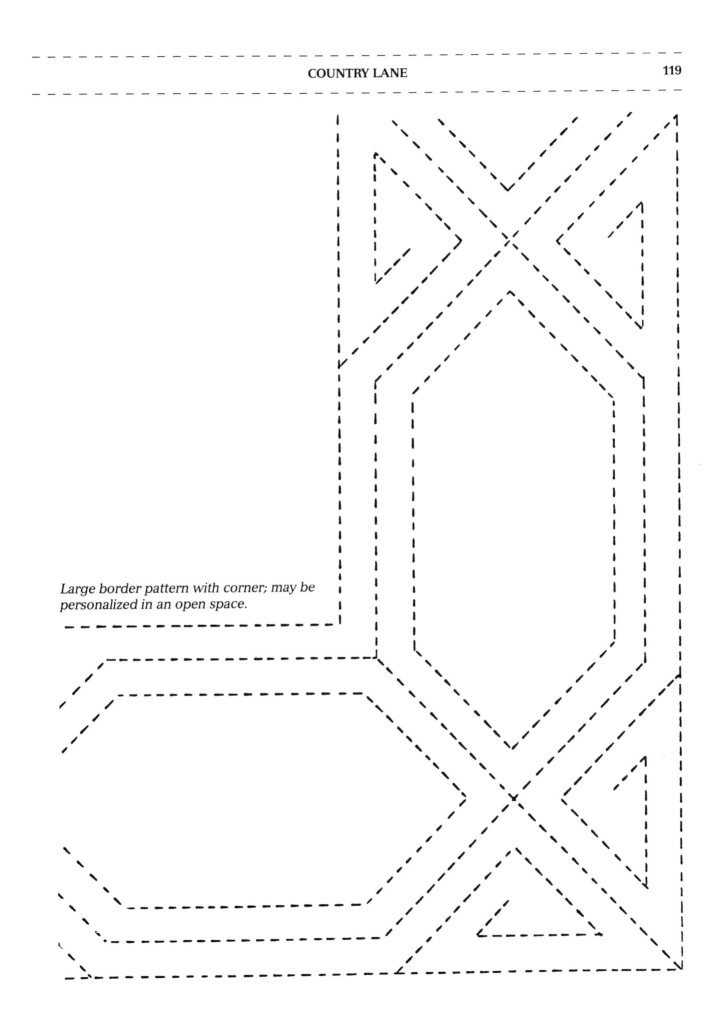

*Large border pattern with corner; may be personalized in an open space.*

# 23. Baroque

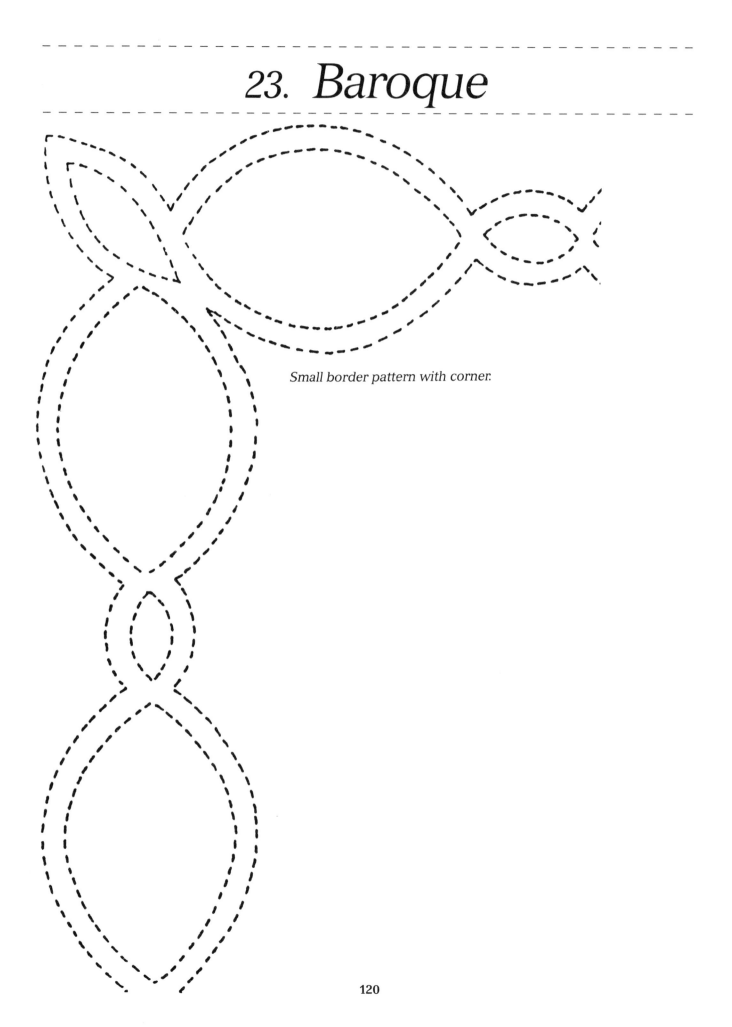

*Small border pattern with corner.*

*Small block pattern.*

*Large block pattern.*

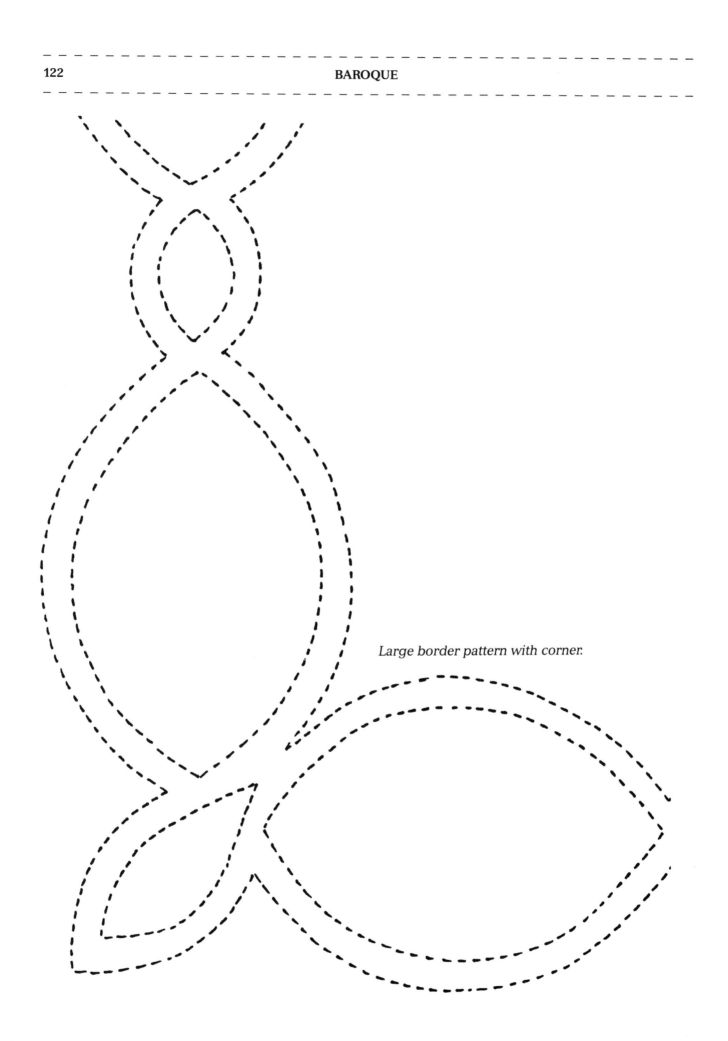

*Large border pattern with corner.*

# 24. Geometric Star

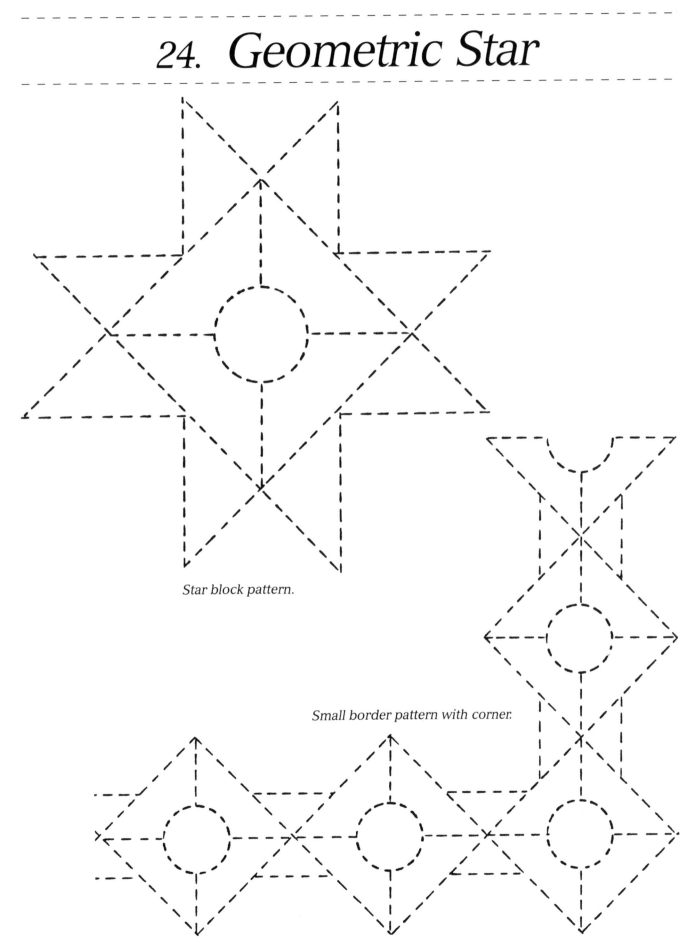

Star block pattern.

Small border pattern with corner.

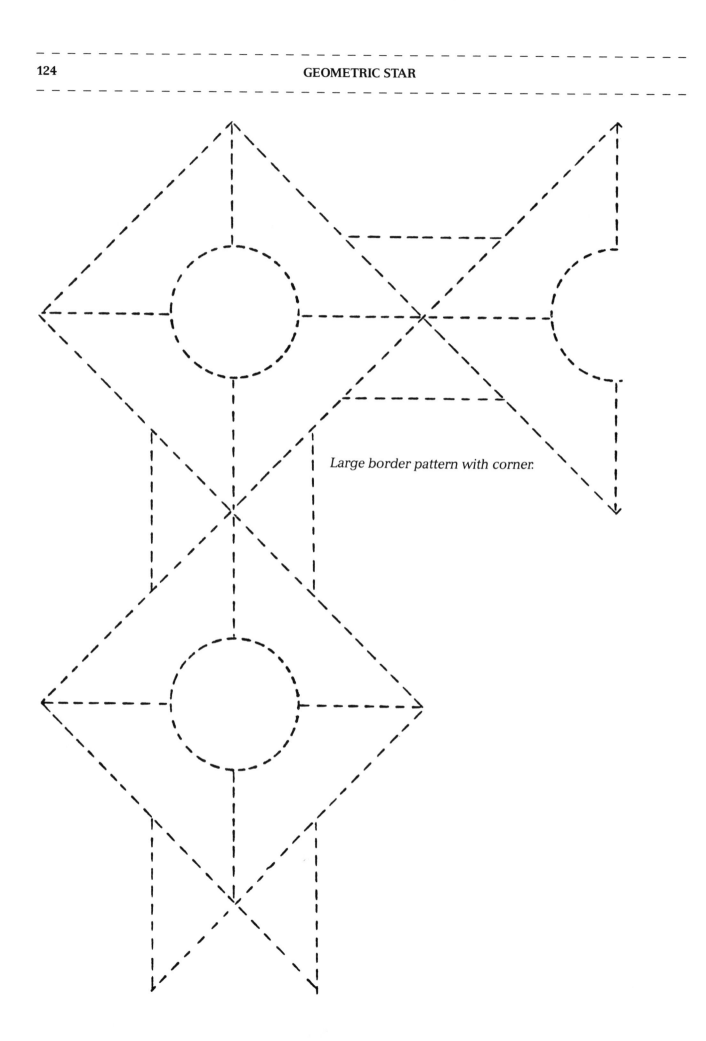

*Large border pattern with corner.*

# 25. Cross Stitches

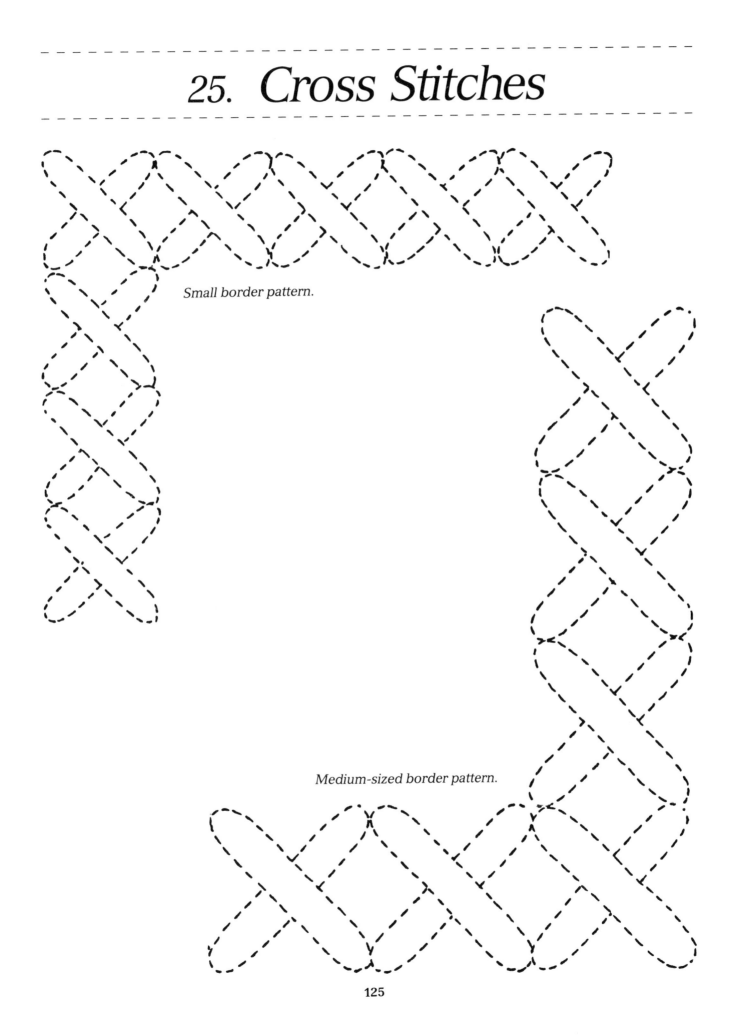

Small border pattern.

Medium-sized border pattern.

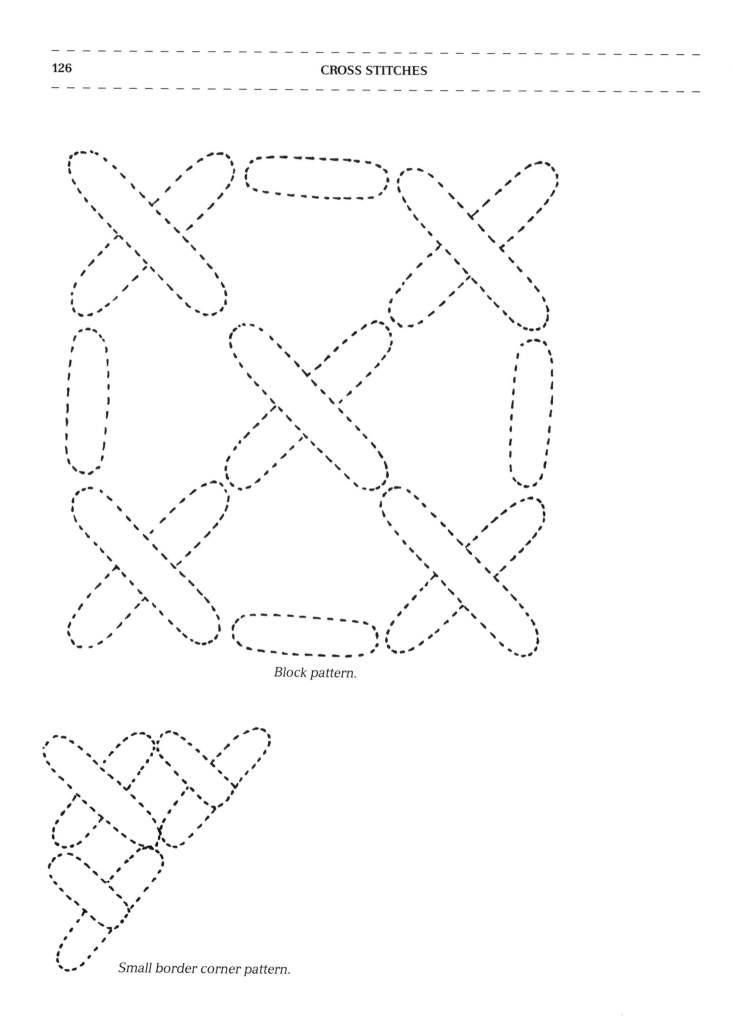

*Block pattern.*

*Small border corner pattern.*

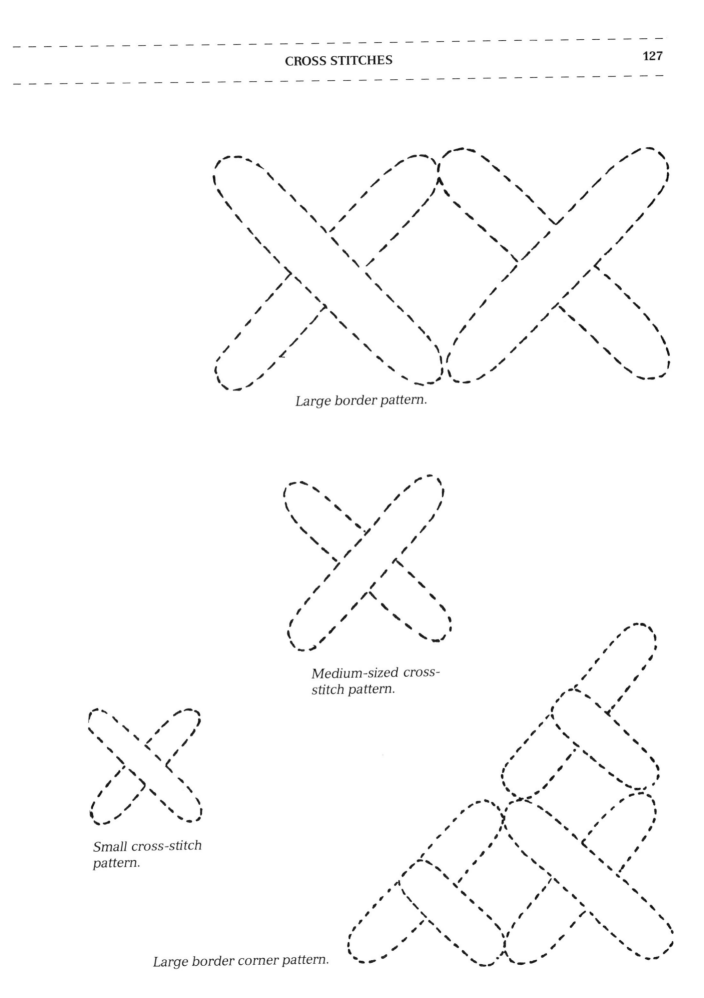

*Large border pattern.*

*Medium-sized cross-stitch pattern.*

*Small cross-stitch pattern.*

*Large border corner pattern.*

# 26. Renaissance Medallion

*Block pattern.*

*Large border pattern.*

*Border repeat.*

# 27. Fleur de Lis

*Fleur de lis block pattern.*

*Border pattern with corner unit.*

# 28. Down in the Deep

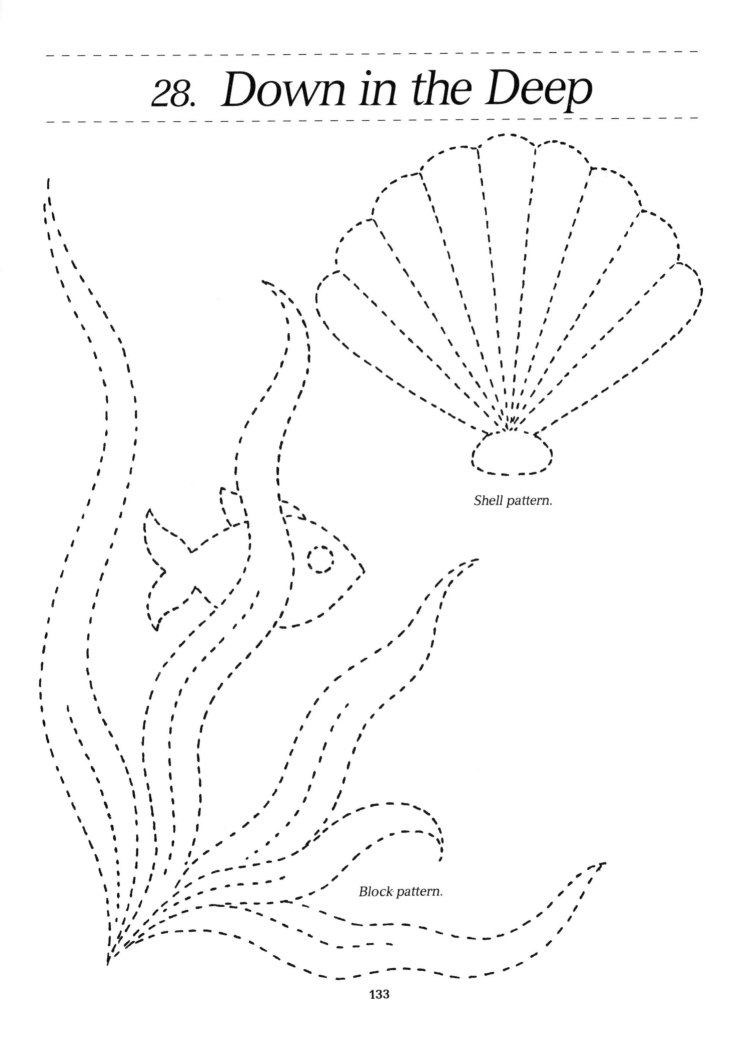

*Shell pattern.*

*Block pattern.*

*Fish pattern.*

*Wave border pattern with corner.*

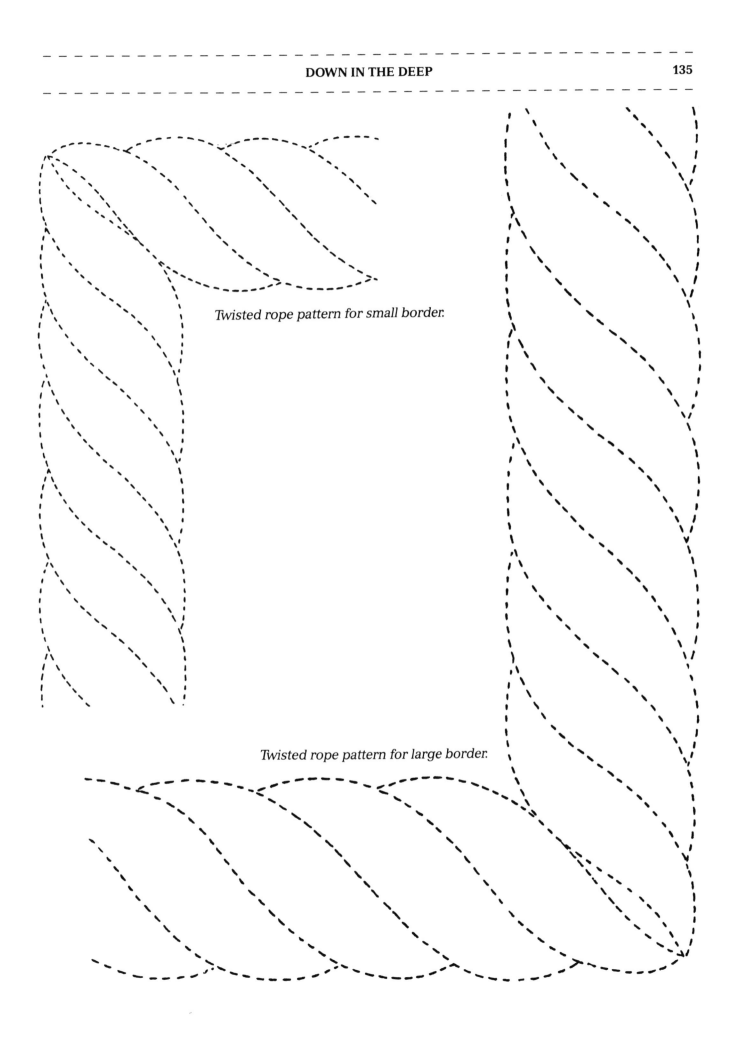

*Twisted rope pattern for small border.*

*Twisted rope pattern for large border.*

# 29. Rose Blossom

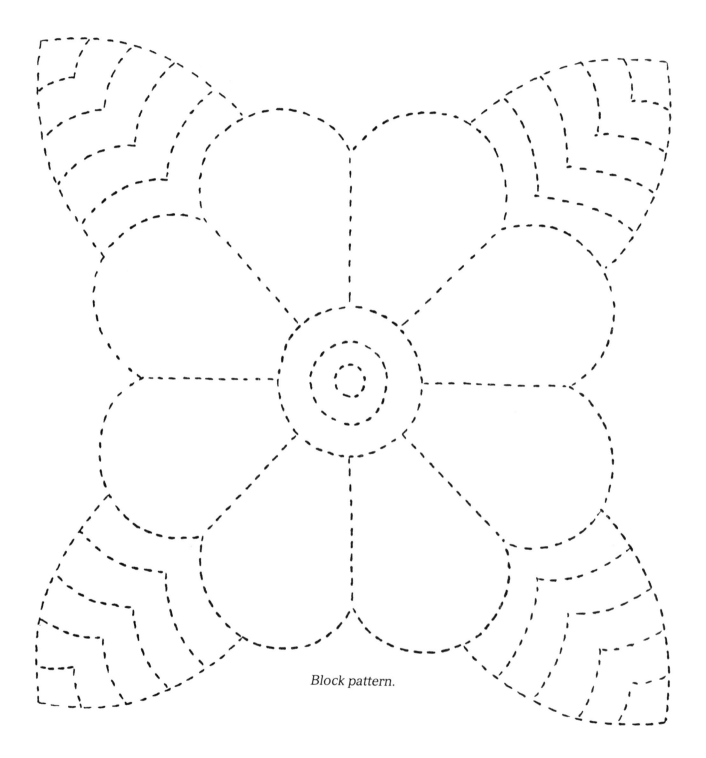

*Block pattern.*

*Border repeat.*

*Block pattern. May be used as a diamond or a square.*

# 30. Teatime

*Teapot and teacup; use for blocks individually; stack them for borders, all of one pattern or alternating.*

*Border repeat.*

*Border pattern with corner.*

# Metric Equivalents

## INCHES TO MILLIMETRES AND CENTIMETRES

*MM—millimetres   CM—centimetres*

| Inches | MM | CM | Inches | CM | Inches | CM |
|--------|-----|------|--------|------|--------|-------|
| ⅛ | 3 | 0.3 | 9 | 22.9 | 30 | 76.2 |
| ¼ | 6 | 0.6 | 10 | 25.4 | 31 | 78.7 |
| ⅜ | 10 | 1.0 | 11 | 27.9 | 32 | 81.3 |
| ½ | 13 | 1.3 | 12 | 30.5 | 33 | 83.8 |
| ⅝ | 16 | 1.6 | 13 | 33.0 | 34 | 86.4 |
| ¾ | 19 | 1.9 | 14 | 35.6 | 35 | 88.9 |
| ⅞ | 22 | 2.2 | 15 | 38.1 | 36 | 91.4 |
| 1 | 25 | 2.5 | 16 | 40.6 | 37 | 94.0 |
| 1¼ | 32 | 3.2 | 17 | 43.2 | 38 | 96.5 |
| 1½ | 38 | 3.8 | 18 | 45.7 | 39 | 99.1 |
| 1¾ | 44 | 4.4 | 19 | 48.3 | 40 | 101.6 |
| 2 | 51 | 5.1 | 20 | 50.8 | 41 | 104.1 |
| 2½ | 64 | 6.4 | 21 | 53.3 | 42 | 106.7 |
| 3 | 76 | 7.6 | 22 | 55.9 | 43 | 109.2 |
| 3½ | 89 | 8.9 | 23 | 58.4 | 44 | 111.8 |
| 4 | 102 | 10.2 | 24 | 61.0 | 45 | 114.3 |
| 4½ | 114 | 11.4 | 25 | 63.5 | 46 | 116.8 |
| 5 | 127 | 12.7 | 26 | 66.0 | 47 | 119.4 |
| 6 | 152 | 15.2 | 27 | 68.6 | 48 | 121.9 |
| 7 | 178 | 17.8 | 28 | 71.1 | 49 | 124.5 |
| 8 | 203 | 20.3 | 29 | 73.7 | 50 | 127.0 |

# Index